Tito

Tito

Neil Barnett

HAUS PUBLISHING • LONDON

First published in Great Britain in 2006 by
Haus Publishing Limited
26 Cadogan Court
London SW3 3BX

www.hauspublishing.co.uk

A CIP catalogue record for this book
is available from the British Library

ISBN 1-904950-31-0 (paperback)

Designed and typeset in Garamond
Printed and bound by Graphicom in Vicenza, Italy

Front cover: akg Images
Back cover: Topham Picturepoint

Contents

*I wish that we had a dozen Titos in Germany,
leaders with such determination and such good
nerves, that even though they were forever encircled
they would never give in.*

Heinrich Himmler

*Turning and turning in the widening gyre
The falcon cannot hear the falconer;
Things fall apart; the centre cannot hold;
Mere anarchy is loosed upon the world,
The blood-dimmed tide is loosed, and everywhere
The ceremony of innocence is drowned;
The best lack all convictions, while the worst
Are full of passionate intensity.*

The Second Coming, W B Yeats

Introduction

The village of Kumrovec, where Josip Broz Tito was born and grew up, is today a half museum. The museum of the 'staro selo' (old village) is in truth a shrine to Tito, given a neutral name to mollify Croatian nationalists who scorn the memory of Yugoslavia and its (Croatian) emperor. In December 2004 Tito's statue, in the garden of the Broz home, house number 20, was dynamited. It has now been repaired, but the culprits have not been caught. Inside the house, meanwhile, is something like an Orthodox iconostasis, a corner dais bearing a heroic portrait of Tito above a bed of fresh red roses. Next to it is a visitors' book, in which every day comments are added in Serbian, Croatian, Slovenian and Macedonian. Some are simply adulatory: 'Tito, we love you.' Others are imploring, such as, 'Tito come back, we need you now.' How can this man, who died in 1980, still inspire such violent and adoring passions?

In some ways Tito *was* Yugoslavia from the Second World War to his death in 1980 and perhaps beyond. He led a communist revolution in parallel with a successful partisan resistance to vastly superior Axis forces and internal opponents. He created a new multinational state and either held it together for longer than any other man could have done, or laid the seeds of its violent demise. He confronted and bested Stalin, and brought his people the most liberty and prosperity in the communist world. He founded something akin to a third camp in the Cold War, at the same time keeping both the Soviet Union and the West in competition for his favour. In all of this Tito's enormous willpower and charisma

The restored statue of Marshal Tito stands in the grounds of his birthplace in Kumrovec, Croatia

were central: like the Sun King, Tito could well say, *l'état, c'est moi*. For this reason, this biography is unapologetically a brief history of Yugoslavia as well as a life of its leader: the two are, in any case, indivisible.

Equally, the more facts are uncovered about Tito, the more enigmatic he becomes. Those who knew him personally often say the same thing. There are many theories about Tito's actions, identity, motivations and background, some of them conspiratorial and outlandish. Many informed and well-educated ex-Yugoslavs believe that the man who led Yugoslavia was not the boy from Kumrovec, but a Russian imposter placed by the NKVD. Others suspect that the split with Stalin in 1948 was staged for some reason. Or that he was a Freemason. The list could go on. But perhaps the most troubling enigma concerns Tito's motivation and aims. No doubt he was in some respects an opportunist and, like all communist leaders, deeply concerned with power. But in the final analysis, the mechanisms of Tito's heart are far more mysterious than those of most of his contemporary statesmen: his mystery only adds to his legend.

Historical background of Yugoslavia

Tito's country, Yugoslavia, is now broken up into five states: Serbia and Montenegro, Croatia, Slovenia, Bosnia and Hercegovina and Macedonia and may yet fragment into six, seven or eight. Yugoslavia dominated the western part of the Balkan peninsula, an area of considerable complexity that has been much misunderstood. Reactions to the Balkans range from dismissal to condemnation: as Bismarck said that the whole of the Balkans was 'not worth the bones of a single Pomeranian grenadier', so the saloon bar bore of the 1990s opined that the Balkan peoples were barbarians best left to their own devices. In French 'balkan' is used colloquially as an adjective to describe barbarity, while in politics and academe 'balkanization' refers to fragmentation, internecine squabbles and finally obscurity. None of this is quite fair or accurate.

But what constitutes the Balkans, or the Near East, or South-Eastern Europe, as the region is also known? Most definitions include the states of former Yugoslavia, plus European Turkey, Albania, Greece, Bulgaria, Romania and Moldova.

Broadly, the region's geopolitical significance well into the 20th century arose from its role of frontier land between the Muslim Ottoman empire and the Christian European empires. 'Turkey in Europe' was a source of anxiety for Europeans who recalled that the Turks had reached the gates of Vienna at the height of their adventures. For Balkan Christians living under the Turks, the peninsula formed the 'ramparts of Christendom'. The line moved many times, and remains a source of conflict almost a century after the demise of the Ottoman empire.

TRIESTE	Country name 1945
ALBANIA	Current country name
·—··—	Country borders 1945 and current
-------	Country borders current

300 kilometres

150 miles

The great diversity and territorial intermingling of ethnic and religious groups was in some ways less of a problem under the Turks than in the context of modern ethnic nationalism. The Ottoman 'millet' system recognized religious communities across the empire (although in an unequal fashion), allaying the need for exclusive and contentious nation states created for one sort of people within a geographic border.

Tito's challenge was recreate a multi-national empire, mostly of Slavs, on a smaller scale. Post-war Yugoslavia barely survived its creator, but to have survived as long as it did was a considerable achievement. The tragedy of Tito is that he lacked the vision or courage to provide for Yugoslavia's continuation in some mutable form – or for its peaceful dissolution.

In the lands corresponding to Tito's Yugoslavia the principal Orthodox Christian groups are Serbs, Montenegrins and Macedonians. Croats and Slovenes are Catholic, as is most of the ethnic Hungarian minority in Vojvodina in northern Serbia. Bosnian Muslims (now known as Bosniacs), Sandžak 'Turks' and the overwhelming majority of Kosovo Albanians are Muslim. In addition to these religious-ethnic distinctions there are linguistic and racial divisions that overlap like the circles of a venn diagram. For instance, the Serbs of Bosnia share a common Slavonian *ijekavski* variant with the Bosniacs, and do not speak the *ekavski* variant of Serbia proper.

Much nonsense has been said and written about the various ethnic groups' supposed visceral, murderous loathing for one another. This arises as much from deliberate nationalistic mythologizing of history as from ignorance. In the case of Yugoslavia, this can be seen in two of Serbia's most significant historical episodes.

On 28 June 1389 an Ottoman army under Murat met the Serbian army of Prince Lazar at Kosovo Polje, near Priština in Kosovo. Murat was trying to expand Ottoman power in the Balkans northwards – in particular to Bosnia – from its footholds in the south. The battle was probably a draw, but some Serbian historians have presented it as a tragedy that lay open the Orthodox peoples to centuries of Muslim domination. Kosovo Polje became the central national myth of Serbia: even in the 20th century Serbian mothers would greet their infant sons, 'Hail, little avenger of Kosovo!' Memories of the myth of Kosovo Polje added much bitterness to the question of Kosovo in recent decades. Not only was Kosovo the cradle of Serbian national pride (and of the Serbian Orthodox church), but the increasing numbers of Albanians in the province were 'Turks' – Balkan people who had converted to Islam under Ottoman rule. In the late 1990s Slobodan Milošević used the widespread belief that Kosovo had been re-conquered by 'Turks' to agitate against the Albanians.

Yet, ironically, Albanians fought on the side of Prince Lazar at Kosovo Polje according to contemporary Albanian and Ottoman accounts. At that time they would have had no political motive for falsely making such a claim.

Similarly, modern Serbian nationalists would like to portray the Ottoman era as one of implacable Christian resistance to the Turk. Yet this is clearly not true. The great Serbian uprising of 1804 under Karadjordje started as an insurrection against corrupt and brutal local Turkish officials. Far from ending Ottoman rule, its objective was to restore the more benign rule of the Sultan; only when the Sultan himself decided to put down such a presumptuous rebellion did Karadjordje find that he was fighting the Ottoman empire: it was never his intention.

After the Serbian uprising, Serbia achieved autonomous status within the Ottoman empire, whose weakness became clearer as the century drew on. In 1878 at the Congress of Berlin the Great Powers rushed into the vacuum created by a feeble Ottoman empire in the Balkans. The Sublime Porte (the Ottoman government) had little choice but to comply with the wishes of its more powerful rivals, and give up Balkan territory.

Before the fall, a gathering of Balkan crown princes; (L to R) Aleksander of Yugoslavia, Boris of Bulgaria, Constantine of Greece, Ferdinand of Romania and Danilo of Montenegro, 1912

Serbia, Montenegro and Romania became nation states, a status Greece already enjoyed. A belt of territory corresponding to Albania, Kosovo, Macedonia, the Sandžak of Novi Pazar (between Serbia and Montenegro), northern Greece and southern Bulgaria remained under the Ottomans. Bulgaria was made a 'principality' still formally under the Turks. Moldova went to Russia. Croatia, Slovenia, Bosnia and Hercegovina, Vojvodina (today the northern part of Serbia) and Transylvania remained Habsburg territories. It was therefore as a subject of Austria-Hungary that Tito was born in 1892 in the Croatian village of Kumrovec.

This rather arbitrary patchwork of nation states, imperial possessions and protectorates served the interests of the Great Powers, who treated the Balkans rather like a chessboard. Austria-

Hungary pushed back the Turks, but did not greatly expand its responsibilities in fractious Slav lands; Russia gained a measure of influence over the Black Sea-Mediterranean corridor, which it coveted for warm-water access; and Prussia believed it had secured a balance among other, potentially hostile powers. But those same powers paid too little attention to the peoples of the Balkans and their national aspirations. The resulting tensions would play an important role in sparking the First World War.

Against this backdrop, Serbian nationalists eyed Bosnia and Hercegovina. In 1908 Austria-Hungary formally annexed Bosnia and Hercegovina, supposedly to suppress violent nationalism. It proved a counterproductive measure. On 28 June 1914 one Gavrilo Princip, a member of the Serbian Black Hand gang, assassinated the Austrian Archduke Franz Ferdinand in Sarajevo. In response Austria-Hungary (backed by Germany) made outrageous and humiliating demands of Serbia, on threat of invasion. Serbia was backed by Russia, in turn allied to France and Britain. Barely a month later Austria-Hungary attacked Serbia, bringing the two great power blocs to war. The First World War was not *about* Serbia or Bosnia – but those Balkan countries, subject to obscure imperial diktats, provided the spark and the kindling.

Tito found himself a soldier in the Austro-Hungarian army, and was taken prisoner on the Dniestr. From there, like the protagonist of a picaresque novel, he found himself caught up in the Bolshevik revolution in Russia.

At the Versailles conference of 1919, Balkan borders were yet again re-drawn. The resulting Treaty supposedly reflected Woodrow Wilson's 14 Points, but self-determination was partially and haphazardly applied. Moreover, in the Balkans it is seldom entirely clear what and who might constitute a state fit to exercise self-determination, and any decision is bound to be contentious, storing up grievances for the future.

A greater Serbia was concocted as the Kingdom of Serbs,

Croats and Slovenes, also including Bosnia and Hercegovina, Vojvodina, Montenegro and Vardar Macedonia. A moderately repressive monarchy imposed Serbian rule on the other nations without recourse to federalism or any other recognition of the diversity of this proto-Yugoslavia. When Tito returned to bring revolution, however, he found few takers. The masses consisted of peasants and smallholders, most of them conservative in outlook, the antithesis of the seething urban proletariat of Marxism. If anything engaged people's passions in this period, it was nationalism. In 1929, after a violent decline in Serb-Croat parliamentary relations, King Aleksander proclaimed a new dictatorial state, Yugoslavia. The Serb-dominated police relied on violence and torture to sustain Belgrade's rule. During this period a radical Croat fascist group, the Ustaše, appeared under the leadership of Ante Pavelić. Pavelić operated from Italy, where Mussolini was plotting the break-up of Yugoslavia. From its earliest years, the recurring motif of Croatian-Serbian tension in Yugoslavia was set.

In 1934 King Aleksander was assassinated in Marseilles by Ustaše gunmen. Pavelić and Mussolini hoped that Yugoslavia would break up, but it endured. Aleksander was succeeded by Prince Pavle, whose prime minister enjoyed warm relations with Hitler: the *Fürher* sought to bolster Yugoslavia as a Balkan ally and breadbasket for Germany.

As Hitler had hoped he would, Prince Pavle joined the Axis powers on 25 March 1941, causing outrage among his people. Two days later the government was overthrown and a new one formed, with King Peter coming of age, and Prince Pavle placed under arrest. Less than two weeks later, a German blitzkrieg swept through Yugoslavia, rapidly taking the whole country. Yugoslavia ceased to exist: the Ustaše were given their own Croatian state, Serbia was occupied and much of the rest was given to neighbouring Axis allies.

Two movements emerged in Serbia to resist the depredations

of the Nazis, their allies and collaborators. These were a royalist militia, the Četniks, and Tito's communist Partisans. The two groups soon began to regard each other as the main enemy, however: the Partisan war was as much a revolution as a resistance to occupation, and the royalists were hostile to such an aim. The Partisans were so successful that Churchill, the romantic conservative, decided to abandon the Četniks and give practical support to the Partisans.

In 1945, with the Germans beaten across the continent, Tito found himself ruler of a new Yugoslavia. From the outset, he sought to avoid the errors of inter-war Yugoslavia and constituted the country as a federal republic with six constituent republics – Serbia, Montenegro, Bosnia and Hercegovina, Croatia, Slovenia and Macedonia – and Kosovo and Vojvodina granted autonomous provincial status.

Most importantly, Tito led a country that had rid itself of the Axis, unlike Poland, Hungary, Czechoslovakia, Romania etc, which had been liberated by the Red Army. This meant that Yugoslavia would have the opportunity to follow a more independent line, and would not necessarily have to be a vassal state of Stalin. Tito set about imposing doctrinaire Stalinist policies at home, while trying to expand his borders in several directions. This independent (albeit hyper-communist) activity disturbed Stalin so much that in 1948 Yugoslavia was expelled from the Comintern.

The country was now stumbling around in a no-man's land of the Cold War. Relations with the West were frosty, while Stalin imposed an economic blockade and intimated invasion. Stalin's death in 1953 coincided with a warming of relations with Tito's wartime supporter, Britain, and by extension the US. As Khrushchev offered reconciliation to Tito, it became clear that Yugoslavia was in a novel and potentially favourable position. While communist, the country was in neither camp of the Cold War, yet on tolerably good terms with both (notwithstanding occasional tiffs). In 1961 this position crystallised into the Non-Aligned Movement, a club for left-leaning developing countries. Yugoslavia was now the inspiration for a third dimension in world politics.

At home liberalisation proceeded in fits and starts, as did the economy. By the 1960s the Yugoslavs enjoyed the best standard of living and the most liberty of the European communist countries. Tito lived and ruled like a king, but was immensely popular among the people – had he decided to underline his rule with free elections, it seems certain he would have won successive polls.

Yet the Croat question continued as a recurring theme, as did Slovenian nationalism. Tito tried to limit Serbian assertiveness, but this was not enough to satisfy other national groups, while at the same time infuriating Serb nationalists. Everyone seemed to view Yugoslavia as a Serbia-plus arrangement, yet perversely, the Serbs managed to see themselves in the perpetual role of the victim. Yugoslavia was an impossible country at best. If Tito's course was not perfect, the immense difficulty of his challenge should be remembered.

Origin

Josip Broz (he would only acquire the *nom de guerre* 'Tito' in the late 1930s) was born on 7 May 1892 in house no 20 in the Croatian village of Kumrovec, in Zagorje, north-west Croatia. There have been many conspiracy theories suggesting that Tito was given the documents of a certain Josip Broz by the Comintern in Moscow to use as a false identity. There has never been any serious evidence to support these theories – they are part of the mystique that surrounds great leaders, especially those who lived conspiratorially.

Undoubtedly Tito's own reminiscences, dictated to his biographer Vladimir Dedijer, make a case for the revolutionary nature of Broz's childhood that at times borders on the absurd. *On one of the hills above Krumovec, towering like a giant, is Cesargrad, the jagged ruins of the medieval castle of the counts Erdödy. They were masters of my village and the surrounding countryside until the middle of the last century, when feudalism was officially abolished in Croatia. They were cruel, and their serfs were often in revolt.*[1] He goes on to describe in some detail a serf revolt in 1573 when *the Zagorje serfs were severely punished. Historians say that the bodies of hundreds of peasants hung from the trees in the villages. It is estimated that during this rebellion between four and six thousand serfs were killed in Zagorje.* His efforts to portray his childhood as a formative time, when he inclined towards revolutionary ideas by experience of oppression, are simply not very convincing.

Much more likely is that he was convinced of the communist cause in Russia during the First World War. There is little sign of such inclinations in his earlier life.

Indeed, aside from the cruelties inflicted centuries before his birth, even by Tito's own account, his childhood was not terribly hard. It probably served his later career as leader of Yugoslavia by giving him insight into the ways of a largely agrarian population, rather than an understanding of seething revolutionary masses.

The Broz family was traditional and conservative. Josip's grandfather Martin was a serf and the last generation of the family to live in the *zadruga*, an extended, clannish and patriarchal family living within a compound. In 1848 – just 44 years before Josip's birth – serfdom ended, along with the rule of the Erdödys, and serfs became peasants.

His father, Franjo, was Croatian and his mother Marija was a Slovene. Josip was the seventh of 15 children, of whom only seven survived. Again he emphasises the hardships of life. *A hard life awaited my parents. Fifteen acres of land, which dwindled as my father's debts came due, were insufficient to feed the family. When the debts became intolerable, the soft and good-natured Franjo gave it up and took to drinking, and the whole burden fell upon my mother, an energetic woman, proud and religious.*[2] He blamed his father's debt problem on the bank of Deutsch and Grünwald, which had bought the Erdödy estate and sold parcels to peasants like Franjo Broz, charging rates as high as 24 per cent on the loans. In Josip Broz's view, the bank was just another incarnation of the Erdödy family. Nothing had really changed.

He also recounts his early resentment of Austro-Hungarian rule, but does not quite extend this to Croatian nationalism . . . *if a Croat went to a station to buy a ticket, he was compelled to ask for it in Hungarian, or be refused. At a nearby village in Zagorje, peasants removed the Hungarian flag from the station. The police opened fire, killing one and wounding ten others. Incidents followed throughout Croatia, in which three thousand people were arrested and 26 killed. As punishment the people had to maintain the Hungarian troops. Four Hungarian soldiers were billeted in our house, and we had to feed them a whole month out of supplies that were not enough for our own meagre needs.*[3] This may go some way to explaining why in 1956 Tito gave his blessing to the Soviet invasion of Hungary.

Kumrovec is a place of great natural beauty, a tiny village set among wooded hills whose successive ranks fade into the haze on a summer day. In other passages he recalls a childhood of Arcadian innocence and contentment, full of practical jokes, dogs, horses, benign grandparents and treats. Apple orchards were raided, gangs of small boys fought inter-village wars and adults told children stories at night around bonfires.

Museum and shrine, the birthplace of Josip Broz Tito at Kumrovec, Croatia

In 1900, at the age of seven he started working on the farm, but was also fortunate enough to go to primary school. The two were not, it seems, exclusive. *I had little time for study. I would go to the meadow with a book in my hand, but reading was out of the question. The cow would drag me by the tether wherever she pleased.*[4] Again, like banks, landowners and the Austro-Hungarian empire, by his own account Broz had an early and vivid initiation into the evils of Catholic church, into which he had been christened. *Once after the [church] service I could not remove the vestments from the big fat priest, who was in a hurry. He was irritated and slapped me. I never went to church again.*[5] Significantly, he reminds readers that the priest was fat – while the Broz family and most other villagers were short of food.

At the age of 12 he left school and started working full-time for his maternal uncle as a cow-herd. This was not well-paid or stimulating work. Three years later Broz went to the little town of Sisak, 60 miles from the village, to work as a waiter. As he says himself, the thought of a smart waiter's uniform and plenty of food was alluring, but the work was a disappointment. So he left the restaurant for an apprenticeship to a locksmith. Broz was given food and lodging in return for training as a locksmith, and twice a week attended a school for apprentices where he studied subjects including languages, geography and history.

He started to learn about trade unions and the relatively left-ist Social Democrats from older journeymen, reading workers' movement pamphlets and collecting donations for the socialist newspaper *Free Word*.

By his own account, at the age of 18 Broz was ready to strike out into the world: *In Croatia, where because of the property qualification only seven percent of the people could vote, the Social Democrats had only one deputy in parliament. In my own village there were only three voters. I was filled with the ambition to do something about these conditions and I was ready to set out from Sisak in the world on my own.*[6] There is little choice but to take Broz at his word (although his complaint about there being only three voters in the village is disingenuous: under Tito there were none).

So at 18 Broz went to work in Zagreb, where he found employment in a metal factory. He also joined the Metalworkers Union and the Social Democratic Party, and participated in marches against low pay. After only two months he returned to Kumrovec. His most important recollection of this return to the village was of a misadventure involving a new suit, a sign of the splendours he would lavish on himself in the future. *I went to a shop and for twenty crowns chose a nice new suit. How joyful I was! I left it at home and went to the shop to say goodbye. When I returned, the door of my room was wide open and there was no trace of my new suit. How sad and dejected I was! I had to go to a second-hand dealer to buy an old suit, for I did not have the heart to return home to Zagorje in the same clothes I had worn when I worked as an apprentice.*[7] For Broz, like many young men of his class at the time, smart clothes were an important source and symbol of pride in defiance of his modest social status.

His stay in Kumrovec was brief, and he soon departed to find work in Ljubljana. When he could not find a job and ran out of cash, he trekked 60 miles across the mountains through the snow to reach Trieste, the great port of the Austro-Hungarian empire. Again there was no work, but the experience of crossing the mountains would later prove valuable in Broz's career as an underground revolutionary.

Broz returned to Zagreb, finding employment with a benevolent mechanic named Knaus. Again, he was active in the union and marched on the streets. Motivated by a desire for adventure and curiosity about the wider world, Broz resigned and set off for Ljubljana with the intention of working in other European countries. This marked the start of a picaresque period of semi-itinerant labour when Broz would learn German and Czech and develop his skill as a mechanic. This period strengthened his confidence, expanded his mental horizons and bred a sturdy self-reliance.

He found work in the Slovene town of Kamnik, again in a metal factory. He joined a vaguely comical 'Soko' (Falcon) group, *a gymnastic organization with an anti-Habsburg platform,*[8] which would often clash with the rival Austrophile 'Orlovi' (Eagles) group. But in 1912 the factory's owners went bust, throwing Broz onto the labour market again.

Here again, his experiences provided him with first-hand, practical experience of what he viewed as a class struggle. Broz and some colleagues heard that attractive wages were on offer at a metal works in the Czech region of Bohemia. But on arriving in the railway station, Broz and his companions were greeted by striking workers who told them that they had been brought in as 'blackleg' labour to break the strike. By forming a common front with the strikers, the Slovene group was able to secure employment at the same time as the management caved in to the strikers' demands. It was a lesson in working class solidarity (although an oddly convenient memory for the later revolutionary Broz – Bohemia at this time seldom suffered industrial or social unrest). Broz started to learn Czech and developed a mutual affection for the Czechs.

But again he remained only two months, eager to see more of Europe and its industrial machine. Several months were spent travelling in Germany and Austria-Hungary, his travels always informed by a fascination for heavy industry. *I remember I was hardly impressed by the Skoda works in Pilsen, because in those days they were obsolescent. I liked the Ruhr much better, with all the smokestacks sprouting like a forest in so small an area.*[9] Again, his recollections seem at odds with reality: the Skoda plant was built around 1900, so it could not have been obsolescent. It was the most modern arms factory in Central Europe, which later armed Hitler throughout the Second World War.

He worked briefly in Pilsen, then for Daimler-Benz in Mannheim.

Broz learned that his brother Martin, who had left Zagorje as a small boy, was working in the railway station at Wiener Neustadt in Austria, and went there to find him. Martin invited his brother to live with his young family, and Broz found work at another Daimler-Benz car factory in Wiener Neustadt, where he had the privileged role of test driver.

This seems to have been a happy period. He would train in the gym, learned to fence and to dance and would spend time in music halls and coffee houses in Vienna. Although he is coy on the subject Broz – who was by this time a fit and good-looking 19-year-old – probably chased girls on his jaunts in Vienna. But while he lived this modest but contented private life, Europe was edging towards war. In 1913, at the age of 20, he was conscripted into basic training in the Austro-Hungarian army in Zagreb to fight for his overlords.

From imperial soldier to Bolshevik

With his country upbringing and practical abilities, Broz was ideal material for a soldier. He also had the successful recruit's knack of both fading into the background in order to avoid trouble, yet at the same time coming to the fore to demonstrate his abilities. As befits the army of a sclerotic and conservative empire, basic training was both humiliating and of limited military value, which Broz despised. His hair was shorn completely by a corporal who said, 'Mister Socialist come here, I'll give you a nice haircut.' The recruits were made to learn the full names and title of the Habsburgs, and were subject to the whims of a despotic corporal who would make a hissing sound when he wanted a cigarette, obliging the whole platoon to run to him with a match. Amidst the endless drill and minor sadism, Broz recalled . . . *it was an old-fashioned and unintelligent army. It operated by rule and formula, and instead of teaching men how to fight taught them how to drill. Worse still, it was an army of oppression, which not only held my people in subjection, but served as an instrument to enslave other nations.*[10]

Yet he flourished. By the end of the year he had achieved the rank of *Stabfeldwebel* (staff sergeant) in the 25th Home Guard infantry regiment, aged just 21, the youngest in the whole army. In the winter of 1913/1914 as the First World War approached he learned to ski on the Sljeme mountains, and took second place in the all-army fencing championships in Budapest.

War broke out following the assassination of Archduke Franz Ferdinand in Sarajevo on 28 June 1914. The assassin was Gavrilo Princip, a member of the secret Serbian Black Hand gang. The

In the hours before his assassination, the heir to the Austro-Hungarian Empire, Archduke Franz Ferdinand, greets dignitaries in Sarajevo, 28 June 1914

independent government in Belgrade had little or no influence over a group of extremist revolutionaries operating on the territory of the Austro-Hungarian empire, but this was the *casus belli* Austria-Hungary and Germany were looking for. In late 1914, following Austria's declaration of war on Serbia, Broz's unit was sent to the Carpathians to prevent the advancing Russians reaching Budapest in support of Serbia.

Despite his leftist leanings, Broz was by no means a fully-fledged communist, and did not heed Lenin's calls to communists not to fight. Initially the regiment was posted to the Serbian front, a fact Tito would later try to conceal. During that time he was arrested and jailed for several days in the Petrovaraždin castle in Novi Sad, capital of Vojvodina to the north of Belgrade. This is an obscure episode. Tito himself claimed that he had been jailed for making seditious remarks, in which he hoped for Austria's defeat or even threatened to defect to the Russian side. *Among the ranks, I spoke out against war. An old sergeant-major, loyal to Francis Joseph, heard of this and betrayed me.*[11] He then claims to have been vouched for by a fellow soldier and released. It seems odd that a senior NCO would be treated in such an arbitrary way and trusted after such an allegation, but nevertheless he was soon with his unit again as it went to the Carpathian front.

Here Broz's company of men from Zagorje was commanded by a Croat, Captain Tomašević. Broz loathed Tomašević for his brutal disciplinary regime, and avenged himself during the Second World War. Tomašević became an Ustaša general commanding Bihać in Bosnia and in 1945 was captured and executed by the Partisans.

The Carpathian front was bloody, miserable and cold. Both the Habsburg and Russian troops were badly equipped (the Russians slightly worse equipped and insanely brave), and a great many men froze to death in addition to those who died from enemy action. Broz hated the carnage and the institutional idiocy of the army, and managed to be given command of a reconnaissance platoon – a dangerous role requiring initiative, élan and intelligence, the reverse of the faceless, meatgrinder warfare the average soldier experienced. He learned leadership, fieldcraft and the use of stealth and surprise rather than sledgehammer force, gaining experience that would prove invaluable in the Partisans. *Night after night [we] crossed the enemy lines and operated deep in the rear. We were very successful and the reason, I believe, was that I took care of my men, saw to it that they were not cheated of their food rations, that they had shoes and the best possible sleeping accommodation.*[12] These are the words of a natural leader.

On Easter morning 1915 his regiment was routed by Circassian cavalry on the Dniester. Broz was run through the back with a two-pronged lance and narrowly avoided being butchered while unconscious by the Circassians when Russians arrived and reined in their excesses.

As a prisoner of war he was taken to the Siberian town of Shvishk on the Volga to recover in an Orthodox monastery. He was very seriously wounded and was close to death at least once. As well as his lance wound he caught pneumonia and typhus, but gradually recovered, learning Russian and reading Russian literature as he convalesced. Unlike some Austro-Hungarian Serbs, Croats and Czechs, he did not volunteer for the Russian army: Broz was interested in revolution rather than romantic Pan-Slavist ideas, and anyway the Croats chose not to identify themselves strongly as Slavs.

Instead he was sent to a prisoner-of-war camp in Kungur to the east, where he was made commander of the 400 inmates, whose task was to work on railway lines. During this time he was beaten by three Cossacks with knouts (whips) at the behest of the camp chief. In the days following the beating he remained in the jail, until one day he heard a commotion outside. *From the distance I heard cries of 'Down with the Tsar'. Armed workers from Kungur, hearing that the Tsar had been overthrown, had come to free the prisoners.*

That meant the revolution in Russia had begun.[13] Yet all was not well – Alexander Kerensky's Provisional Government wanted to continue the war, and faced a challenge from the Bolsheviks, who wanted to withdraw, an enormously popular idea in a country that had suffered five million war dead. Broz was thrown back into jail, then sent again to work on the railways.

Once more in the mould of an adventure novel, he escaped by stowing away on a goods train to St Petersburg, arriving days before the July demonstrations against the Provisional Government. These escapades echo Churchill's escape from the Boers, suggesting a powerful will and sense of adventure, something quite out of the ordinary run of men: as Djilas wrote, 'From the start, from early youth, Tito refused to accept the fate of being one among many. The war and the Russian Revolution, with Communism growing in both, were the forms and the realities, the dreams and the visions, through which he realised himself.'

In St Petersburg Broz found himself on the stage of history. Over three days in July Bolshevik workers tried to unseat the Provisional Government, Broz among them. During a demonstration he was caught in a fusillade fired by government troops, and decided to flee Russia for Finland. But he was arrested *en route* and thrown into the dungeons of the Peter and Paul Fortress for three weeks, thence to Siberia. But once again, he escaped, fooling a guard on the train back to Kungur. On transferring to another train he found himself in Omsk, and learned from the local Red Guard of the Bolshevik success in St Petersburg. *'This is the Soviet government!' exclaimed a worker. The October Revolution had started that day, and the armed workers were Bolsheviks from Omsk.*[14] In his discussions with Dedijer he was remarkably modest about his time in Russia. *It has been written on many occasions that I took considerable part in the October Revolution and the civil war in Russia. Unfortunately, that is not so. I served several months in the Red International Guard, but I never fought at the front . . .*[15]

While Broz was in Omsk Russia descended into civil war. The Bolsheviks had many enemies. The Social Revolutionaries (SRs) wanted to continue fighting the Germans by all possible means, and found that the Allies were prepared to support them. Britain, France, America and Japan intervened, sending troops into Russia in support of the SRs and the White Guards under General Kolchak. The Allies wanted to keep Russia in the war, but also to throttle the beast of Bolshevism.

In July 1918 the anti-Bolshevik Whites and the Czech Legion overran Omsk. The Red Guards were too few to resist, and went to ground, fearing brutal treatment if they surrendered. Broz found refuge in the home of the Belusov family, who were sympathetic to the revolution. Here he met 15-year-old Pelagea Belusova, a beautiful blonde girl who possessed great spirit and intelligence. He did not remain long in the Belusov house, but remembered Pelagea, whose name he shortened to Polka.

Broz then went out into the country near Omsk, and met a nomadic Kirghiz chief, Hadji Isaj Djaksembayev, who claimed descent from Ghengis Khan. Djaksembayev employed Broz as an engineer at his water mill and hid him from the Whites. The two men became friends, but Broz found Kirghiz ways not entirely to his liking. He told

The story of the Czech Legion is among the oddest of the Russian Revolution. The 70,000 Czech soldiers had deserted from the Austro-Hungarian army, some on 'Pan-Slavist' grounds with the intention of joining the Tsar's army, others inspired by the Czech leader Jan Masaryk's, fight to persuade the Allies to break up Austria-Hungary. After the Bolshevik withdrawal from the war they were put on trains to get them back to the Western Front, where they could fight on the Allied side. But during the journey fighting broke out between the Czechs and some Bolshevik Hungarians, resulting in the death of a Czech and a Hungarian. As a result, the Czechs made a fractious alliance with the Whites and became a formidable anti-Bolshevik force.

Zilliacus, *Every now and again {the women} would dig down in their clothes, fetch up a great grey louse and crack it between their teeth so that they were all bloody as though they had been smeared with lipstick. It used to make me sick – I could not eat my food.*[16]

While Broz was in the company of the Kirghiz, a radically changed post-war Europe was emerging. In November 1918 Germany's Kaiser fell, to be replaced by a Social Democrat government, effectively ending the war.

The Kingdom of Serbs, Croats and Slovenes (SCS) was declared on 1 December 1918 under the Prince Regent Aleksander Karadjordjević. The country was a hastily-constructed thing, however, and its borders and constitution were not clear at this stage.

As the new Balkan borders were thrashed out at the Paris conference the next year the Bolsheviks, ironically, indirectly contributed to the relatively impressive size of SCS. In 1919 the Comintern was formed to extend the communist revolution around the world. Lenin believed that some of Russia's prisoners of war could be sent back to bring revolution to their own countries. Tito, given time, would do just this. But a Hungarian prisoner, Béla Kun, had much swifter success. His short-lived Hungarian Soviet Republic of 1919 was in reality a disaster for Hungary: the Allies did not want a revolutionary upstart at the Paris peace conference in that year, and so Hungary (already on the losing side of the war) was not invited. Hungary would be reduced to a rump.

Hungary's loss was its neighbours' gain. SCS as decided at the Conference comprised something very similar to the Yugoslavia Tito would rule, that is Serbia and Montenegro plus the former Austro-Hungarian possessions of Croatia, Bosnia and Hercegovina, Slovenia and Vojvodina, plus the former Ottoman possessions of Vardar Macedonia and Kosovo. However, the Serb-dominated government allowed Italy to take parts of northern Croatia, and for the Italian poet Gabriel D'Annuzio to be granted an independent state in the town of Rijeka (Fiume in Italian).

This dismayed Croats enormously, adding to their chagrin at being ruled by what most of them saw as a Serb government.

Serbia had fought bravely and steadfastly on the Allied side during the war, enduring huge losses, and had been raised to the status of hero nation by British propaganda. Consequently, the Allies deemed Serbia to be a suitable overlord for the Western Balkans, and the beneficiary of Austria-Hungary's disintegration. In one way this was sensible, as Serbia had been *de facto* independent for over a century, possessed the institutions of a state and was the largest of the south Slav nations. In another way it was a disaster in waiting because the new SCS was unitary rather than federal and made no allowance for the aspirations of the non-Serb nationalities, namely Croats, Slovenes, Montenegrins, Macedonians and Kosovo Albanians. Just as the Versailles Treaty was a long fuse for the detonation of the Second World War throughout Europe, so it primed the Western Balkans for years of strife and bitter internal conflicts that it would suffer after 1941, not to mention the two domestic terrorist groups that would emerge in the inter-war years.

In 1919 Broz returned to Omsk to look for Polka, but found the family gone. He eventually found her walking down a street in a neighbouring village. Having declined the offer to marry a daughter of Hadji Isaj Djaksembayev, he now decided to marry Polka. The two revolutionaries wed in a full Orthodox service in Omsk in 1919.

He decided to return with Polka to his homeland, now SCS. In 1920 he joined the Russian communist party according to sources such as Djilas (although Tito never said this himself). It was long believed in Yugoslavia that he had been recruited as an agent of the Comintern, but this was never proven. The question is slightly academic – Comintern agent or not, Broz was now a convinced Bolshevik bent on bringing revolution to his homeland.

Return to the Balkans

On returning to his homeland, Broz found much changed in the almost six years of his absence. Whereas before he was a subject of the Austro-Hungarian empire, now he was a subject of the Kingdom of Serbs, Croats and Slovenes. In Kumrovec he found that his mother had died, and he was unable to find work. With Polka pregnant, it was imperative that he found employment, but the economy was in a dire state. He worked briefly in a factory in Zagreb, then as a waiter. Eventually he found a job managing a flour mill in Veliko Trojstvo to the east of Zagreb. The owner, Samuel Polack, was Jewish, and he and Broz established a warm relationship. He remained in this backwater for four years, but there were not uneventful years – they were the beginnings of his revolutionary career.

The new unitary monarchy of the Kingdom of Serbs, Croats and Slovenes was an affront to the non-Serbs, particularly Croats, and there had been violence in Montenegro over the declaration of in December 1918.

Moreover, the new monarchy was sclerotic and corrupt from the outset. Nikola Pašić, the Radical nationalist leader, was prime minister. He was a devious, Byzantine man in his late seventies whose two principal enthusiasms were power and Serbia. He therefore devoted his energies to staying in power and to extending Serbian hegemony in the region. King Aleksander was essentially a robber baron, milking the state funds and setting up businesses including production of *šlivovic* (plum brandy, the favourite Serbian firewater), wine and vegetables, all tax-free thanks to his status as monarch. At the same time, he worked to limit the power of the Constituent Assembly, a weak parliamentary body, in order to retain as much power as possible for himself.

Although they were at odds on many issues, the prime minister and the king were united in facing down two phenomena that threatened both of them — non-Serb nationalism and communism. In practice, this meant establishing a near-dictatorship.

Following the Constituent Assembly elections in 1920, a year before the constitution was promulgated on 28 June 1921, the interim government had outlawed the Communist Party of Yugoslavia. The Communists' election successes had alarmed them. Two communist terrorist attacks further hardened the government's line, one narrowly missing the King, another killing the interior minister.

The Croat Republican Peasant Party (HRSS) of Stjepan Radić boycotted the parliament on the grounds that it was no more than a polite excuse for Serbian domination. After Radić agreed to ally his party with the Red Peasant League, the HRSS too was banned. Until Radić's extraordinary decision to join the Serb Radicals in a coalition government in 1925, there was widespread repression in Croatian regions.

For Broz, as a Croat (although not a Croatian nationalist) and a Communist, this meant frequent clashes with the state. But at first it seems Broz was isolated from other communists. Then one day Stevo Šabić, a Comintern agent who had been recruited in Russia as a prisoner of war, visited him in Veliko Trojstvo. Broz and Šabić received instructions to collect weapons in preparation for an uprising, and buried some rifles, pistols and grenades near the village. The uprising never came, and the weapons were not unearthed until the Partisans needed them in 1941.

With the party in tatters after the government's crackdown, a split emerged. A moderate camp hoped to persuade the government that they could function as a normal parliamentary party,

Stalin disbanded the Comintern, the organisation intended to spread revolution throughout the world, at the height of the war in 1943. In a statement received by Tito and the Partisans during the German Fifth Enemy Offensive, he said, 'it puts an end to the lie that 'Moscow' intends to interfere in the life of other countries and 'Bolshevise' them.' Keeping the wartime alliance together had become more important than international communism – something Stalin had never, in any case, been a great enthusiast for. Its replacement, Cominform, was never to assume the role of revolutionary exporter, and was instead a club for communist states.

and thereby have the ban lifted. A more radical faction believed that the ban demonstrated that violent revolution was the way forward, and that representation in parliament was no more than distraction from their revolutionary aims. Broz was firmly in the latter group, an aggressive revolutionary, impatient with idle plotting and eager for action. *The working masses wanted to fight, as they showed us during the municipal elections held during the same year . . . I gave a lecture in the headquarters of the Zagreb trade unions and ended with the cry; 'The workers can conquer only with the help of arms!'* he told Dedijer.[17]

In a party riddled with secret police informants, Broz's party activities did not go unnoticed. In 1924 he was elected to the district committee. That year he gave a speech at the funeral of a communist, and then laid a red flag over his coffin. To do this, Broz had been obliged to gatecrash the Catholic funeral the man's family had arranged. The infuriated priest reported Broz to the police, who clapped him in irons with another suspect and paraded them through the streets. After eight days in jail, they were tried but found innocent thanks to the prosecuting attorney, a member of the Orthodox church given to virulent anti-Catholicism.

None of this much bothered Samuel Polack, the mill owner, and he was content for Broz to be a communist as long as he worked well. But when Polack died his son-in-law Oskar Rosenburg inherited the business. Rosenburg and Broz did not hit it off, and Rosenburg was disturbed by the gendarmes' frequent searches of Broz's room. He told his employee, 'Either you go in for politics or you work.' Broz was too proud to tolerate such an ultimatum, and left.

In the autumn of 1925, at the behest of the party he moved to the shipbuilding town of Kraljevica in northern Croatia. From his own account, Broz's arrival in this hive of industrial activity was not accidental: *From the first day of my arrival, I assumed the task of organizing a trade union branch. A few weeks later the elections for shop stewards were called and I was among those elected. After getting to know the shipyard workers, I restored a Party organization which police terror had disbanded for many years.*[18] In 1926 he organized a successful strike over late payment of the workers, which succeeded in its aims, but also resulted in Broz being sacked.

He went to Zagreb and found a job at the nearby railway wagon factory in Smerderevska Palanka, where again he came into conflict with the management. If Broz's accounts are to be believed, it is not hard to see why industrial unrest could easily be stirred up with the right leadership. In an article he wrote for the Zagreb *Organized Worker*, he described how the factory would advertise for dozens of skilled workers, but then not offer employment once they had come the 40 miles to the plant from Zagreb, instead telling them to wait for work outside the factory. *Every working man here should be aware that that the management does this merely to have as many unemployed workers as possible at the factory gates, to frighten the others.*[19] Men would work up to 16 hours per day, and the factory was bitterly cold in winter, so that some of the men developed pneumonia.

Broz's shop steward work, as well as the article, got him sacked once more. Another job in a Zagreb workshop ended in a similar way. But just as Broz was attracting the hostile attention of employers and the secret police, he was being noticed in party circles. He was appointed Secretary of the Metal Workers' Union in Zagreb. It was 1927 and a crucial moment when he became a professional agitator and revolutionary.

Days later the secret police 'invaded' the union offices and threw Broz into jail. He was accused of having plotted a revolution while at the Kraljevica shipyards along with six other workers. While in jail in the town of Ogulin Broz kept busy by radicalising his cellmates, mostly common criminals. One day there was a town meeting outside the jail, and as the Prefect said, 'Long live His Majesty King Aleksander!' a young cellmate of Broz shouted out of the window, 'To hell with the king!' Broz instructed everyone to pretend to be asleep and in the investigation that followed, it was impossible to determine the culprit.

Broz's next project was a one-man hunger strike *against the system prevailing in the jail*. After five days he was promised his main demand, a trial, and he resumed eating. The prosecution case turned out to be flimsy, resting on the dissemination of some communist tracts. Broz was found guilty and given four months, but was released pending appeals by both the prosecution and the defence. Instead of appearing for the hearings, however, he went underground in the guise of a respectable middle-class engineer so that he could continue his work and avoid the possibility of a jail sentence.

Back in Zagreb, he resumed his union work, also taking on the post of secretary of the Leather and Processing Workers' Union. During this time the police came down harder than ever on communists as the economy slumped and unemployment climbed. Broz's passion for orthodoxy and loathing of 'factionalism' was emerging: *The leadership of the Communist Party at that time, instead of concentrating all its powers in the struggle for a better life for the workers and peasants, was sunk in a struggle between the left and the right factions, a conflict not of principle but merely career struggle for Party positions . . . in the local party organization at Zagreb there was a strong group of workers who were against both these factions. It was clear that without unity there could be no future for our work.*[20] These words reveal a ruthlessness towards internal dissent that would culminate with the Adriatic gulag of Goli Otok in post-war Yugoslavia: dissenters are enemies and must be dealt with as such.

Of course, in the mafia-like world of communism, that gave the standard-bearer of orthodoxy a convenient right, even a duty, to eliminate rivals. And as George Orwell showed in *Lear, Tolstoy and the Fool*, being *right* led Communist leaders to confer frightening powers on themselves.

Happily for Broz, his sentiments were shared in Moscow. As early as 1922 the Fourth Congress of the Comintern attacked the Yugoslavs for 'factionalism',[21] and again in the two following years for 'deviations to the right and deviations to the left'. In Moscow there was a witticism: 'two Yugoslavs, three factions'. The Comintern also sought to break up the Kingdom of Serbs, Croats and Slovenes in order to break up a country allied with France, an 'imperial outpost': local communists were ordered to seek 'self-determination to the point of secession'. In his later career Broz would work to unify the Yugoslav nationalities, but at this point he was still a footsoldier of communism, and obeyed Moscow's wishes, speaking out against the kingdom.

Obedience and ambition ran in parallel in the communist party. In 1928 Broz was elected Zagreb Branch Secretary of the party after he proposed the dismissal of the existing committee and direct leadership by the Comintern. He immediately sent a quite chilling letter to the Executive Committee of the Comintern urging liquidation of *fractional strife in the Communist Party of Yugoslavia*. At a time when the world communist movement centred on Moscow, Broz had the breadth of vision to see beyond local squabbles and develop his standing with the Comintern.

He remained incognito for fear of arrest for the Kraljevica sentence, always looking over his shoulder, carrying a revolver and never spending more than a few nights in one bed. On May Day 1928 he was arrested during rioting and jailed for 15 days. But the police fell for his false identity and did not realise that he was Josip Broz.

Sooner or later his luck was likely to break, and on 4 August 1928 it did. The police, acting on a tip, were waiting for him at a rendezvous with a fellow conspirator. He was roughed up and interrogated, then jailed for three months to await trial. In that time he mounted another hunger strike and smuggled newspaper articles out of jail.

At the trial in Zagreb the prosecution alleged, 'Josip Broz did throughout the years of 1921 to 1928 in Zagreb and other places, as a member of the illegal Communist Party of Yugoslavia, carry out Communist propaganda in so far as he organized members of that Party . . . he organized and became a member of an association which has as its declared purpose the propagating of communism and illegal, forcible seizure of power.' The prosecution also claimed that Broz had two bombs hidden in his quarters. He claimed at the trial and subsequently that the bombs had been planted by the police.

Broz delivered a text-book performance for a Communist in a 'bourgeois' trial. He told the Presiding Judge, *I admit that I am a member of the illegal Communist Party of Yugoslavia and I admit that I have propagated Communism. I tried to point out to the proletariat all the injustices done to them. But I do not recognize the bourgeois Court of Justice because I consider myself responsible only to the Communist Party.*[22] He refused to explain the meaning of some of the Comintern cipher codes found in his notebook and would not give up his comrades.

Beyond these formulaic phrases, his charisma riveted the court. The conservative *Novosti* reported, '[Broz] is undoubtedly the most interesting person in the trial; his face makes one think of steel. His shining eyes look over his spectacles in a cool but

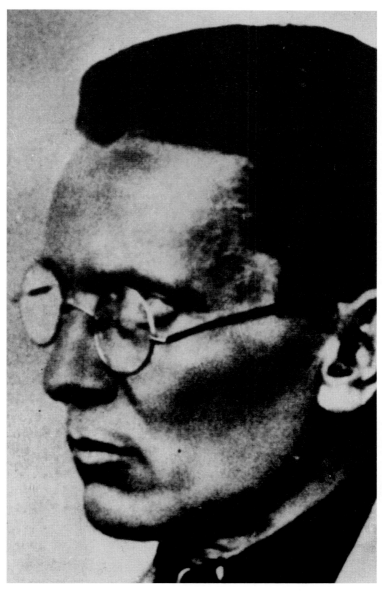

Hard labour: an early photograph of Tito taken on his release from prison in 1933

energetic way . . . A large number of spectators no doubt knew the stubbornness with which he maintains his beliefs, for a silent attention reigned in Court throughout the hearing.'[23]

As he was led out of the court he shouted, *Long Live the Communist Party of Yugoslavia*. He received five years' hard labour.

The ambitious revolutionary

In 1928, at the age of 36, Broz disappeared into Lepoglava jail for five years. Daily existence in jail was not particularly unpleasant and the regime was fairly humane. His technical abilities were put to use in the prison power plant, which earned him privileges including access to books. Here he met Moša Pijade, a Jewish intellectual jailed for distributing Communist propaganda, who became his ideological mentor. *It was*, he told Fitzroy Maclean, *just like being at a university*.[24] The freedom of movement that came with the technical work allowed the two to organize a Communist group in the jail and even to have occasional meetings outside the walls of the jail.

If Broz was able to make the best of his time in jail, he paid a heavy price in his personal life. Since returning from Russia, Polka had borne five children, only one of whom, Žarko, survived. Little is known about the state of their marriage, but clearly Broz's five-year sentence presented problems. Not only would Polka have to provide for herself and Žarko in a country whose language she still spoke haltingly, but her marriage to Broz potentially put her at risk. One day they disappeared without saying a word to anyone. They had gone to Moscow. This would not be the last of Polka, but it marked the end of the marriage in any meaningful sense.

The country saw great change while Broz was in jail. After a Serb parliamentarian shot dead the Croat leader Stjepan Radić, King Aleksander proclaimed a new dictatorial state through a *coup d'état*, on 6 January 1929. The Kingdom of Serbs, Croats and

Slovenes was dead and Yugoslavia was born. The change of name signalled that from now on, there would be less tolerance than ever of Croatian nationalism. The Vidovdan constitution was suspended, as was parliament, severe censorship was imposed and all political parties were banned. The Serb-dominated police increasingly fell back on violence and torture to sustain Belgrade's rule, particularly against Croatian nationalists and Communists. Two of Broz's future closest collaborators, Edvard Kardelj and Aleksander Ranković, were arrested, tortured and jailed. In the same year the world economy dived after the Wall Street crash. Yugoslavia was no exception, and the worsening economic conditions exacerbated the country's political crisis.

The Party buckled under the assault. In the hope of preserving a leadership cadre, the Comintern instructed senior members to flee to Vienna and continue their work as émigrés.

In many parts of Europe fascism arose in direct confrontation to Communism. In 1933 Hitler's Nazi party came to power. In Yugoslavia a Croat fascist group, the Ustaše, appeared under the leadership of Ante Pavelić, seeking the destruction of the Yugoslav state and an independent Croatia. Pavelić operated from Italy with the enthusiastic backing of Mussolini, who was plotting the break-up of Yugoslavia with an eye on some of its territory. The Ustaše worked through terror and assassination. It was allied with another violent separatist group, the VMRO of Macedonia, which mounted a bloody resistance to Belgrade's 'Serbianization' programme. From Yugoslavia's inception, the recurring motif of simmering and sometimes violent Croatian-Serbian tension was set.

As the political climate deteriorated, Communist prisoners were denied remission. Broz had no hope of release before 1933. In the event he was made to serve the four-month sentence he had evaded for the Kraljevica charges in 1927, and emerged from jail in March 1934. As a condition of his release he was told that he must live in Kumrovec where he must remain and report every day to the police. Most people in the village were delighted to see him, the exception being Father Noivak, who according to Broz told his congregation that the Antichrist had returned to Kumrovec.

Soon he left Kumrovec to resume his underground work in Zagreb, where the party was getting back onto its feet. To avoid the police he dyed his hair red, wore spectacles and grew a moustache and adopted several *noms de guerre* such as 'Zagorac'. To close comrades he was known as 'Stari' (the old man), but at this point he started using 'Tito'. He had a brisk way of giving orders, pointing and saying, 'you, this', or in Serbo-Croat, *'Ti, to'*, and some sources claim this is how he earned the name. Tito's own explanation is more prosaic: *I took it as I would have any other, because it occurred to me at the moment.*[25] Either way, Tito was born.

Having been safely locked up during worst of the police terror, Tito avoided the fate of so many senior Yugoslav communists: death, torture, long prison sentences or émigré life in Vienna. Like Stalin in pre-revolutionary Georgia, he found himself in the prestigious position of a middle-ranking Communist living underground while the leadership worked in exile. His moral and political standing within the Party and in the eyes of the Comintern could benefit greatly if he played his hand well and managed to avoid arrest.

The Zagreb Provincial Committee chose Tito to go to Vienna and establish a working linkage between the leadership and those who remained underground. As in his youth, he crossed the mountains on foot: this time it was to avoid the border guards, not for lack of funds. He arrived tired and bruised in Austria on 25 July 1934 only to be stopped by a group of armed youths. *I had no idea what he wanted until I looked at his sleeves, whereupon I was no longer in doubt. They wore red armlets with the swastika. Chancellor Dolfuss had been assassinated that day, and the Austrian Hitlerites were attempting to seize power in the whole country.*[26] It was a close encounter with the enemy. He managed to pass himself off as an Austrian and continue to Vienna.

The leadership *fell on me like bees on honey* for news of Yugoslavia, and after a few weeks in Vienna Tito was appointed to the Central Committee, with the task of organizing a conference for all of Yugoslavia. On his return, he was the most senior Communist inside the country.

He started, too, to build a cohort of close allies loyal to him, including Edvard Kardelj and Boris Kidrić, Aleksander Ranković and Milovan Djilas, men who would help him in the struggle and later play important roles in Tito's government. For them, Tito was an inspiring leader, according to Kardelj: 'We found him very direct of speech and manner. He was in his early forties, about twenty years older than we were, and looked it. But he was nothing like the old Party leaders. When you asked him a question, he didn't always come back with a quotation from Marx, Engels or Lenin. Instead, he spoke in practical, common-sense terms.'[27]

In October 1934 King Aleksander was assassinated in Marseilles by a joint Ustaše/VMRO plot. Prince Pavle (Paul) assumed power, ruling as regent until the boy King Peter came of age. Tito had been at liberty just seven months. Life in Yugoslavia became yet more perilous for Communists, as it was under the pro-fascist Schuschnigg government in Vienna, so the Committee decided to send him to the Comintern in Moscow.

For Tito, aged 42, it was an emotional return to Russia: *For us it was the homeland of the workers, in which labour was honoured, in which love, comradeship and sincerity prevailed. With what joy had I felt the strength of the country as, emerging from prison in 1934, I listened in the dead of each night to Radio Moscow and heard the clock of the Kremlin striking the hours, and the stirring strains of the International.*[28] In reality the USSR was descending into hell under Stalin's paranoid rule.

King Aleksander of Yugoslavia and the French Foreign Minister, Jean Louis Barthou, moments before both were assassinated in Marseilles, 1 October 1934

Foreign revolutionaries were accommodated at the Hotel Lux in Gorki Street. Tito's survival during this period was a remarkable achievement. East European communists who were suspected of ideological deviations, being too headstrong, or who had the bad luck of being denounced were hauled off in the night by the NKVD, never to return. Béla Kun, the leader of the short-lived Hungarian Soviet Republic of 1919, the second successful revolution after Russia's, was among those executed. . . . *There were no end of arrests, and those who made the arrests were later themselves arrested. Men vanished overnight, and no one dared ask where they had been taken.*[29] This must have been disturbing at the very least, but Tito said that to acquiesce in the NKVD's sprees was a *revolutionary duty*. There has been speculation that he survived because he was denouncing others, but this slur has never been substantiated, and until Russia decides to open its secret police files it will remain pure speculation. It is equally likely that he was saved by his experience of army life – where diligence and an ability to avoid antagonizing superiors is a great asset – and his practical rather than ideological leanings.

He was appointed to the secretariat of the Balkan section of the Comintern and given the work name 'Walter'. Also he gave lectures, read widely (especially on military subjects) and was trained in revolutionary warfare by the Red Army. He was treated to a tour of the collective farms and factories of the USSR and would occasionally visit the opera or the ballet.

Polka, who had abandoned Tito when he was in jail, was in Moscow. But there was no reconciliation, and she was probably living with another man. What is not clear is who initiated their divorce in 1936. Tito started a relationship with one of the staff of the Hotel Lux, an Austrian Communist named Lucia Bauer (real name Johanna König), and they married in October 1936. For some reason Tito covered up his marriage to Lucia Bauer and erased it from official records of his life. This may be because he was ashamed of having betrayed Polka, or conversely because he felt humiliated by Polka's betrayal. Either way, Bauer was wiped out of the records, and it is almost certain that Polka's name was deliberately blackened. A biography by Phyllis Auty published in 1970 is typical: 'Tito found that after Polka had returned to her native land in 1929 she had made other associations in the Soviet ruling class. She no longer considered herself as Tito's wife, and let their son run wild, to be brought up by another woman.'[30] Auty does not mention Lucia Bauer.

Afterwards, for his entire life, Tito would wince or become enraged if Polka's name was mentioned. Djilas wrote: 'Nothing is known about the relationship between husband and wife [Polka]. That is not accidental because for Tito any reference to that marriage was painful. It seemed as if he wanted to blot out every trace of it from his life and his memory.'[31]

In early 1935 Tito returned to Yugoslavia to lead the party inside the country, while the Yugoslav Politburo moved from fascist Vienna to Paris. He started moving between Yugoslavia, Moscow and Paris using false identities. In Paris he set up an office to facilitate the movement of Yugoslav volunteers for the Spanish Civil War, and acted as a link between the leadership and the underground, as before. Inside Yugoslavia he acquired a near-legendary status as an underground Comintern agent whose hand was suspected in every outbreak of industrial strife. In Moscow, still staying at the Hotel Lux, survival must have been the most pressing matter, for this was the period of Stalin's great purges. There was also savage repression of communists in Yugoslavia: Tito was in constant peril.

The leader of the Yugoslav party, Milan Gorkić, was summoned to Moscow in August 1937 and executed. The previous year Gorkić had bungled the transport of 1,000 volunteers from Yugoslavia to Spain, resulting in the loss of a chartered ship and the arrest of hundreds of volunteers on the Montenegrin coast. Tito himself had doubted Gorkić's loyalty, wondering why so many communists travelling on passports supplied by Gorkić were captured. After the demise of Gorkić he was given temporary charge of the Central Committee, then formal leadership in late 1937. He said, perhaps a little disingenuously, *I had no ambition to take over the leadership of the Party, and never had. But I did want the leadership to be strong, firm and revolutionary. I had never thought of becoming the head, but I did want the head to be a man who could work.*[32] Yet Tito must have felt uneasy or somehow ashamed by his route to the leadership, for in conversations with his biographer Dedijer, he glosses over Gorkić's execution.

Finally he was free to impose his will on the Party. The Central Committee returned from Paris to Yugoslavia; factions were dissolved; Moscow subsidies were rejected; the Party was extended throughout Yugoslavia; and there was a new emphasis on indoctrination. In the guise of 'new men', Tito's own closest comrades – Kardelj, Ranković, Djilas, Končar and Ribar – were placed in senior positions.

The task of strengthening the Party in Yugoslavia gave Tito a good excuse to stay away from the clutches of the NKVD in Moscow. In 1938 a purge of Yugoslav communists in Moscow claimed over 100 scalps, and both Polka and Lucia Bauer were arrested, potentially compromising Tito, although eventually both women were released. There were several other close calls with the NKVD, such as when an old adversary, Petko Miletić, denounced him. Tito was exonerated, but Miletić himself was arrested and disappeared shortly after.

As Stalin tore apart the leadership of European Communist parties, threat from the Nazi Germany intensified. In 1938 Britain and France agreed to let Hitler take the Czech Sudetenland. Stalin's initial policy was to form a temporary common front with bourgeois democracy against fascism. Yet Prince Pavle was turning towards Germany under the influence of his pro-Nazi prime minister Milan Stojadinović, and was convinced that France, his ally in the Little Entente, had no intention of defending Yugoslavia. Stalin, however, went several steps further and entered the Molotov-Ribbentrop or Nazi-Soviet Pact on 23 August 1939. On 16 September Germany invaded Poland.

Prince Regent Paul of Yugoslavia bids Hitler farewell after a visit to Germany,
1 January 1940

This *volte face* caused ideological mayhem among the Yugoslav communists.

Several European parties declared that they would defend their countries against Hitler regardless of the Pact. What followed was an embarrassing and humiliating series of somersaults designed to mollify Moscow, where Tito was trying to discern Stalin's policy. *We accepted the pact like disciplined Communists, considering it necessary for the security of the Soviet Union . . . but the Soviet-German pact did not for a moment weaken our vigilance in preparing for the defence of our homeland in the event of attack.*[33] Doublethink was an essential skill for a communist who wanted to survive and indeed to remain sane. But it is interesting to consider that Tito, as a proud and intelligent man, must have felt some sense of private anger at these moments, and that this perhaps influenced his later rebellion against Stalin.

In 1940 Tito returned from Moscow and after a series of evasive manoeuvres around the Mediterranean in which he was nearly caught several times, returned to Zagreb. Here he lived with a Slovene girl, Herta Hass, who was also a communist.

In October he organized the Fifth National Conference in Zagreb. By his account the Party was now 12,000 strong with a 30,000-strong communist youth movement. The imminence of the threat to Yugoslavia was plain, and he used the conference as a call to arms, closing with the words: *Comrades, we are faced by fateful days. Forward for the final struggle. We must hold our next conference in a country free from aliens and from capitalists.*[34] He could clearly see the simultaneous war and revolution to come, and relished the prospect.

Invasion, Resistance & Revolution

As Tito's communists set about defining their ideological position on the rather confusing Soviet-Nazi-imperialist manoeuvrings of the early war, Yugoslavia remained neutral as the Nazi menace gathered around it. By early 1941 the Wehrmacht was sweeping through the Balkans as Hungary, Romania and Bulgaria joined the pro-Axis 'Tripartite Pact', and Greece appeared in the Nazi's gunsights. As Yugoslavia's position became increasingly beleaguered, Hitler presented Prince Pavle and his government with both carrot and stick. Should they join the Tripartite Pact voluntarily, Yugoslavia would receive the port of Salonika (today Thessaloniki), which implied that it would keep Macedonia, a territory jealously sought by all its neighbours. Should Yugoslavia refuse this offer, there was an unspoken but obvious threat of invasion and occupation.

The government finally agreed to join the Tripartite Pact on 25 March 1941, with little enthusiasm and with as much neutrality as could be salvaged. There was widespread outrage on the streets, particularly in Belgrade, and patriotic air force officers, encouraged by America and Britain, overthrew the government just two days later. Prince Pavle and his government did not resist the coup, and Crown Prince Petar was declared King, with the coup leader, General Dušan Simović, leading the government. The coup was heroic and doomed in equal measure. Days later, perhaps seeing the hopelessness of their position, the new government decided it would adhere to the Tripartite Pact, but the reversal was in vain. Hitler became enraged and ordered an invasion under the codename 'Operation Punishment'. It began on 6 April with a massive aerial bombardment of Belgrade, followed by a blitzkrieg on several fronts that Yugoslavia was powerless to resist.

The Germans and Italians set about dismembering Yugoslavia. Ante Paveli´c's fascist Usta˘se were given their own Croatian Quisling state (including Bosnia and Hercegovina), which was called the Nezavisna Država Hrvatska, or the Independent State of Croatia (NDH), split between German and Italian areas of occupation. Pavelić assumed the title *poglavnik* (like *Fürher*). Slovenia, parts of Dalmatia, Kosovo, Vojvodina, Montenegro and Macedonia were carved up between Germany and its allies Italy, Bulgaria, Hungary and Albania. The remaining rump Serbia was occupied by the Germans and nominally placed under the leadership of a Pétain-like collaborator, General Milan Nedić.

On the day the German attack started Tito was living in Zagreb. Four days later he issued the following proclamation to the public: *You who are struggling and dying in this battle for independence, be convinced that it will end in success . . . Do not lose heart, close your ranks and do not bow your*

Pavelić's Ustaše regime set up concentration camps for Serbs, Jews, gypsies, homosexuals and opponents of the regime. In the most notorious, at Janesovac, victims were knifed and clubbed to death in their thousands. Elsewhere men, women and children were driven over cliffs. According to an Italian journalist who interviewed Pavelić, he had a basket containing 40 pounds of human eyes in his office, 'a present from my loyal Ustaše.' The regime's attitude to the Serbs was simple: 'kill a third, convert a third (to Catholicism), expel a third.' Yet it is often forgotten that their popular support was minimal, with some studies placing it as low as 5 per cent. In truth, the Ustaše relied heavily on the support of German and Italian occupiers, the latter increasingly unwilling and sometimes hostile to the Ustaše as the war went on.

heads under the heavy blows you are suffering.[35] But in reality there was little resistance, and what resistance existed was disorganised, and certainly not communist-inspired. Days later the government capitulated and fled.

Tito remained underground in Zagreb and then Belgrade in the guise of Slavko Babić, engineer, initially unable or perhaps unwilling to resist an occupier that was still an ally of the USSR: Moscow sent home the Yugoslav ambassador on the grounds that Yugoslavia no longer existed. In this demoralising situation, Tito called an underground meeting of the Central Committee in Zagreb in April, which nevertheless decided in principal on a broad national resistance to the invaders.

Yet still after three months there was no organised communist resistance, supposedly because of the need to arm and prepare. That changed overnight on 22 June when Germany launched Operation Barbarossa, the invasion of the USSR. Resistance was now in the USSR's direct interest, and the CPJ obligingly roused itself.

As a telegram from 'Walter's' controllers in Comintern ordered, the resistance was to be as much a flank operation for the USSR as a national liberation war for Yugoslavia: 'Absolutely essential that you should take all measures to support and alleviate the struggle of the Soviet people . . . Start a partisan war in the enemy's rear.'

Tito duly issued a written proclamation: *The hour has struck to take up arms for your freedom against the fascist aggressors. Do your part in the fight for freedom under the leadership of the Communist Party of Yugoslavia. The war of the Soviet Union is your war, because the Soviet Union is fighting against your enemies . . . Do your proletarian duty unfalteringly and with discipline. Get ready now for the last and decisive battle.*[36] The Partisans had been called to arms under Tito's generalship.

Partisans started attacking railway lines and supply columns, sabotaging telephone lines, publicly burning collaborationist newspapers and attacking German soldiers wherever they were isolated. These were mostly random actions, but on 4 July Tito issued a plan for a more organized resistance. The manifestations of the government of the 'old Yugoslavia' were a prime target, particularly the police, whose armouries were also to be plundered. From the country Partisan detachments would launch hit-and-run raids on the towns, never trying to hold ground, in the tradition of the Balkan *hajduk*, a rebel-cum-bandit from Ottoman times. The haste of the German occupation meant that there were few occupation forces outside the main towns, allowing Partisans to roam with relative freedom.

During the second half of 1941 the rising spread throughout Serbia, Montenegro, Bosnia and Hercegovina and parts of Croatia. German reprisals were savage: official policy laid out the killing of 100 local male civilians in response for the killing of one German, but this only drove more people into the Partisans.

A German administrator wrote this message to Berlin, revealing profound confusion in the face of the Partisan rebellion: 'All our attempts to canalise these people in a constructive direction and separate them from the Communists have failed and had to be abandoned . . . The people just do not recognise authority . . . They do not believe in anyone any more and follow the Communist bandits blindly . . . Some go so far as to prefer Bolshevism to occupation by our own troops.'[37] Tito, with Moscow's prodding, realised that the Partisans should lead a national resistance that was not limited nationally or ideologically. While leadership and the underlying aims of the Partisans were resolutely and fanatically communist, its public face was quite different, reflected in the formal name of 'National Liberation Partisan Detachments'. This pan-Yugoslav army would, Tito saw, form the solid bedrock for a united communist Yugoslavia after the war.

In September Tito left his underground existence in Belgrade and moved to 'liberated' territory in the mountain village of

Tito photographed in the early Partisan resistance

Stolice near Užice, to the south of the capital. Overstretched and under-manned as resources flowed to the Eastern Front, the Germans had given up manning the garrison in Užice in the face of incessant Partisan attacks, and the town became known as the 'Užice Republic'. There was a railway, a party newspaper named *Borba* (Struggle), a postal service, schools, a 'people's court' and a rifle factory turning out 400 weapons per day. Užice, like other liberated areas in Bosnia, Montenegro and Croatia, was ruled by 'peoples' committees'; an embryonic Communist state was being built under the Germans' noses.

Near to Užice in the Ravna Gora the Četniks, a conservative and narrowly Serbian resistance movement, were operating under Colonel Dragoljub 'Draža' Mihailović. During the opening months of the war Tito and Mihailović tried several times to agree on joint command or at least formal co-operation. But the ideological gulf between them was too wide: the Četniks

The Četniks (officially known as the Yugoslav Home Army) were a conservative, royalist Serbian nationalist resistance movement under the leadership of Colonel Dragoljub 'Draža' Mihailović. They were often bearded, hung with bandoliers and knives and fond of *šlivovic* (plum brandy). Their flag was a skull and crossbones emblazoned *Svoboda ili Smrt* (Freedom or Death). But they were cautious, aiming to preserve Serbia and its fighting potential until a promising moment came for a full-scale rising. Local Četnik commanders started to make accommodations with the enemy that increasingly became outright collaboration, leading to conflict with the Partisans. Tito's victory over the Četniks was completed in 1946 when the new government executed Mihailović for collaboration and war crimes. A rival, openly collaborationist group led by Kosta Pećanac was also known as 'Četniks', but was quite distinct.

wanted to conserve the system and people of Serbia, while the Partisans wanted to create a new Yugoslavia at any cost. While Tito took the very Russian and Marxist view that 'worse is better', the Četniks were often deterred by German reprisals against civilians. The Partisans were becoming the most ruthless and effective resistance movement in Yugoslavia, each day bringing more recruits, weapons and supplies. Soon coexistence would turn to skirmishing and then outright conflict between the two forces.

At the same time, ethnic violence broke out: Yugoslavia was entering a civil war. The Ustaša started to commit atrocities against Serbs, driving many Serbs and some Croats into the ranks of the resistance movements. Bosnian Muslims joined the Ustaše, massacring Serbs, while many Muslims were killed by Četniks. As a matter of policy the Germans were utterly brutal towards civilians. In Kragujevac in central Serbia between 2,000 and 5,000 men and boys were slaughtered in a day in October in retaliation for a simultaneous Partisan–Četnik raid on the town of Gornji Milanović.

In November the Germans finally moved against Užice in what the Partisans termed the First Enemy Offensive, with three divisions of German reinforcements supported by aircraft, armour and artillery advancing on the town. Realising his Partisans had no hope of holding ground in the face of a mechanised army, Tito gave the order to withdraw southwards through the mountainous Sandžak and into eastern Bosnia. By December the liberated areas were no more and the civilian population was left to face terrible reprisals by the Germans.

At this point the outside world believed that the Četniks were leading the resistance to the occupation, while Tito and the Partisans remained relatively

In July 1941, the Italians declared that Montenegro would become an Italian principality. On 13 July the Montenegrins attacked the Italians; those who were not killed or captured sought refuge in a handful of garrisons. But the wild exuberance of the rising could not make up for poor co-ordination and discipline, and counter-attacks reversed most of their gains. The Communists among them were immoderate, and as a result, by autumn the Četniks started to co-operate with the Italians, and Axis propaganda about crazed Bolshevik Partisans began to ring true. After the war Tito spoke of the 'harsh, sectarian and incorrect attitude' of the Montenegrins, mistakes he learned from and tried not to repeat during the rest of the war.

obscure. During the First Enemy Offensive Radio Moscow, broadcasting in Serbian, reported that the Četniks were the main force of resistance. Vladimir Dedijer recalls, 'Tito stood still, aghast. I had never seen him so surprised, either before or after that day. He merely said: *But that's impossible.*'[38] The British, too, were under the same impression, and sent an officer to liaise with the Četniks.

The attack on Užice started a pattern of massive offensives by the Germans and their allies. Tito's response was to concede ground and spread the revolt to new areas, denying the Germans a target to strike at while remaining always on the offensive.

As Sergeant-Major Broz of the Austro-Hungarian army, Tito had learned well how to lead small, lightly-armed detachments on raids and reconnaissance missions, an experience that gave him crucial insights as a military leader. Yet Milovan Djilas – a senior Party member and Partisan leader whom Tito subsequently imprisoned twice – knew him well and wrote that he had, 'a great concern for his personal safety' and was a mediocre military leader.[39] But even Djilas concedes that Tito was an inspirational political leader in wartime, and it was Tito's determination to resist, his charismatic personality and his skilful mixing of Communism with patriotic rhetoric that drove the Partisans throughout Yugoslavia.

Equally, it is hard to deny the audacity, moral leadership and nerve Tito displayed as a commander when under immense pressure from the enemy. As the Partisans withdrew from Užice to Rogatica in the Bosnian mountains in December, the situation appeared bleak. It was painfully cold, there were no leaves on the trees to provide cover from view, many of the wounded had been captured and killed, and food, weapons and ammunition were in short supply. Yet Tito never faltered in maintaining morale. Among the items he chose to haul over the mountains under German fire was a consignment of 5,000 copies of *The Short History of the Communist Party* in Serbo-Croat. That month Tito formed an élite unit, the First Proletarian Brigade, which soon expanded to five brigades. (This piqued Moscow, where any overt sign of ideological fervour was seen as a threat to the new Soviet alliance with Britain and America.)

Just a month later another offensive came, but the Partisans managed to slip the noose and escape into the Jahorina mountains to the south, setting up headquarters in Foča. This set a pattern of cat-and-mouse whereby the occupiers would mount an offensive and the Partisans would melt away – often with considerable losses – into another part of Yugoslavia to spread the revolt.

Tito and Koča Popović during the Partisan campaign

During the winter of 1941–2 the Italians and the Četniks, who by now widely collaborating with the occupiers, continually harried the partisans in Montenegro, so that Tito decided to incorporate them into his force in eastern Bosnia. But there, equally, cover, food, arms and ammunition were in short supply. Seizing the initiative and forestalling the inevitable German spring offensive, in May he decided to move his Partisans into Croatia and take the fight into the heartland of the NDH.

During June the core of the Partisan forces pushed northwards through Italian- and German-held territory, while elsewhere – in Dalmatia, Serbia, Slovenia and eastern Croatia – the Partisans harassed the occupiers and their quislings. There were, by their estimates, at least 150,000 men under arms. But unlike the parochial and loosely-organised Četniks, this was a disciplined and mobile force willing to fight the enemy anywhere in Yugoslavia without compromise.

In November 1942 they overran the town of Bihać in the north of Bosnia amid a considerable stretch of liberated territory. Here on 26 November they first convened the Anti-Fascist National Liberation Council of Yugoslavia (AVNOJ), a provisional national government in all but name. Grandpapa (Tito's Comintern controller) sent the following: 'Do not fail to give your Committee an all-national Yugoslav and all-party anti-fascist character, both in its composition and its programme. Do not look on the Committee as a sort of government, but as the political arm of the struggle for national liberation.'[40]

Therefore, Tito exercised restraint. The state's communist nature was veiled, and instead the Council spoke of a socialist federal state where all nations and outlooks would find a home. It did not describe itself as a provisional government.

The respite was short-lived, and in January 1943 a huge new German offensive named Operation *Weiss* (or the Fourth Enemy Offensive) bore down on the Partisans in Bosnia and Croatia. Some of the best units of the Werhmacht and the SS, backed by Ustaše, Četnik and Italian troops, attacked from three directions. Tito's response, as ever, was movement and offensive action: *We must avoid fixed fronts. We must not let the enemy force us by clever tactics on to the defensive. On the contrary, the spirit of our troops must be offensive, not only in the attack, but in defence as well. During an enemy offensive the offensive spirit must find expression in vigorous and audacious guerrilla tactics, in operations behind the enemy's lines, in the destruction of his communications, in attacks on supply centres and on cases which are temporarily weakened.*[41] Spirit, or morale, was the Partisans' best and only answer to German firepower.

But the Germans' ring of steel failed thanks to the Italians' reaching their positions late, and the main Partisan force escaped over the Neretva river into Montenegro and eastern Bosnia. From there they wreaked destruction on the Četnik blocking force to the south.

By now Hitler was becoming increasingly infuriated by the situation in Yugoslavia. Not only was a band of Slav irregulars defying the Reich, but the failure to secure the Balkan peninsula opened up opportunities for the Allies to strike into occupied Europe. After a desperate winter in Russia, and facing a major confrontation with the British in North Africa, this was not what the *Fürher* needed. He wrote to Mussolini in February: 'It is both impressive and alarming to observe what progress the insurgents have made with their organisation. We are only just in time to suppress the rebellion if we are not to run the risk of being stabbed in the back in the case of an Anglo-Saxon landing in the Balkans.'[42]

Tito was, in other words, making a significant contribution to the wider effort against the Nazis, not least by tying up fighting units that would otherwise be deployed to the Eastern Front. As Hitler's letter suggests, a new offensive, Operation *Schwarz*, was in preparation. The Partisans now found themselves in exactly the area they had evacuated the previous year because it was easily encircled, sparsely populated and lacking food. Tito decided to break south-east into Kosovo, again taking the battle into a new area.

Before he could do this the Germans sprung Operation *Schwarz* in late May. German-led forces numbering 100,000 attacked a concentration of 20,000 Partisans from all points of the compass. But again the Partisans found the slightest chink in the cordon, slipping across a half-demolished bridge over the Šutjeska at Suha on 6 June. Still the offensive continued, with artillery and air power pounding the fleeing Partisans as the infantry closed in on them. While sheltering from shellfire, Ranković said, 'never have we been in a worse situation.'[43] Six days later the First Proletarian Brigade, Tito's original élite formation, smashed its way through the main German line on the Kalinovik-Foča road, allowing other Partisan forces to flow through the gap

A BRAVE PEOPLE FIGHTING FOR THEIR HOMES AND LIBERTY
NEED YOUR HELP TODAY
PLEASE GIVE GENEROUSLY

By courtesy of the proprietors of " Punch."]

FREEDOM ON THE HEIGHTS

[In admiration of the mountain guerilla army still fighting against Germany and Italy on Yugo-Slav soil.]

2d. each

A poster on behalf of the Yugoslav Relief Society first published in *Punch*.
1 May 1941

into the relative safety of the woods beyond. Once more the Partisans found respite as they moved into eastern Bosnia, but the series of offensives had taught Tito a lesson: from now on, there would be less concentrations for the enemy to strike at, and instead a broader, yet more elusive front. But, despite losing thousands of men, it was clear that by surviving as a fighting force, the Partisans were winning against overwhelming odds.

My Enemy's Enemy

Tito's Partisans were the basis of a new Yugoslavia – multinational, disciplined and above all, Communist. Whereas the Četniks were parochial in their outlook and areas of operations, the Partisans' ranks contained all of Yugoslavia's peoples and were mobile, fighting for an ideological end rather than a village. There was fierce discipline – unlike the often-drunk Četniks, drinking was forbidden. When the Partisans needed food from the local population, they paid for it, and if a Partisan was discovered taking something by force, he was shot. There were many girls in the Partisans, but 'fraternisation' was strictly forbidden. Partisans who 'fraternised' were executed if discovered, yet Tito was not without female company during the war.

This is not to say there were not moments of levity. Fitzroy Maclean recalled an evening on the Dalmatian island of Korčula: 'I have hazy memories of the dance at a village called Blato which rounded off our day's entertainment and which was dramatically interrupted by the explosion of a small red Italian hand grenade which became detached from one of the girls'

In 1937 Tito met Herta Hass, a Slovenian communist, who became his 'common law wife', a circumlocution to mollify a puritanical party. Like his Russian wife Pelagea, Herta was both strikingly beautiful and younger than him. Shortly after giving birth to a son, Miša, Tito betrayed Herta with Dovorjanka Paunović, always known as 'Zdenka', who posed as his secretary when they were in the field. Herta was captured by the Ustaše, and released in an exchange of prisoners in 1943, only to learn that she had been usurped, for which she never forgave Tito.

belts as she whirled round the barn in which it was being held. That night we slept very soundly.'[44]

Maclean went on, ' . . . all of them, young, and old, men and women, intellectuals and artisans, Serbs and Croats, had been with him "in the woods" since the early days of resistance, and had worked underground with him before that, sharing with him hardships and dangers, set-backs and successes. This common experience had overcome all differences of race or class or temperament and had forged between them lasting bonds of loyalty and affection. They had, in short, become comrades in the deeper, non-political sense of the word.'[45]

But despite their great achievements, since the order had come from Moscow in 1941 to 'Start a partisan war in the enemy's rear', the Partisans had received not one rifle or any other equipment from the USSR. This was not for lack of asking; at the height of the Fifth Offensive Tito sent the following encrypted message to his Comintern controller, 'Grandpapa': *Am obliged once again to ask you if it is really quite impossible to send us some sort of assistance? Hundreds of thousands of refugees are menaced by death from starvation. Is it really impossible, after twenty months of heroic, almost superhuman fighting, to find some way of helping us? We have been fighting for twenty months without the least material assistance from any quarter.*[46]

Generally the replies were infuriating to Tito, doubly so since Radio Moscow insisted on promoting the Četniks as the main resistance force, and the Comintern refused to believe that they were actively collaborating with the Germans and Italians. Most of Moscow's messages either contained platitudes or ideological directives that must have seemed particularly irrelevant in the thick of fighting.

Tito's patience did not always hold. During the Fourth Offensive he signalled in response to a typically unhelpful message: *If you cannot understand what a hard time we are having, and if you cannot help us, then at least do not hinder us.*[47] At times the Russians

Tito, commander of the Partisans, in 1942

actively damaged Partisan morale, as when old Moša Pijade, Tito's former cellmate, spend 37 nights on a freezing Bosnian plateau waiting for a Soviet supply flight that never arrived. On learning that no supplies would come, some of the Partisans wept.

Moscow's attitude towards the Partisans was driven in part by a fear of offending the US and Britain. As the USSR waged total war in defence of its homeland, the new and unlikely alliance with the Western allies was of infinitely greater importance than a Communist-led insurgency in the Balkans. If Washington and London believed that the Comintern was spreading revolution into Europe under the cover of the struggle against Germany, it could jeopardise the entire alliance.

To forestall this, Stalin disbanded the Comintern at the height of the war in 1943. In a statement received by Tito and the Partisans during the Fifth Offensive, he said, 'it puts an end to the lie that "Moscow" intends to interfere in the life of other countries and "Bolshevise" them.'[48] Keeping the wartime alliance together in order to protect the USSR and its revolution had become more important than international Communism – something Stalin had never, in any case, been a great enthusiast for.

Moreover, Stalin possibly feared the rise of a charismatic and independent rival Communist leader with a strong domestic base.

The Western allies, for their part, were committed to the royalist government-in-exile in London, and in turn to their resistance force, the Četniks. But the British were starting to receive intelligence reports and decrypts suggesting that Partisans had been much underestimated and might be worthy of support. Churchill, eager to find a way to exploit the 'soft underbelly of Europe' authorised a joint Military Intelligence-Special Operations Executive (SOE) Military Mission under Captain Bill Deakin to clarify the situation.

Deakin and five others parachuted into Bosnia to join the Partisan headquarters at Mount Durmitor at the height of the Fifth Offensive. An earlier liaison officer to the Četniks had been in contact with the Partisans, and an observer, Major William Jones, had followed, but this was the first formal Mission. At this stage the British knew very little about Tito, and Deakin did not realise that he was head of the CPJ.

Tito and Deakin formed a personal bond, which was in part no doubt genuine, but which also served Partisan purposes very well. During an airstrike on an exposed mountain ridge Deakin saved Tito by pushing him into a trench. Tito and Deakin were wounded, while Tito's dog and another British Captain were killed.

Deakin, sharing the hardships of life with the communists during the offensive, accepted Tito's word on his ambitions for Yugoslavia. He reported, 'The Partisan leadership has no plan or intention of immediate social revolution. The prime object is the construction of the country after the war and it is realised that revolutionary action will cause internal struggles which will fatally weaken the country.'[49] Conversely, he reported that the Četniks had been in 'close, constant and increasing' collaboration with the Germans.

While there is no doubt that Churchill, Deakin and others simply wanted to discover who was the most effective opponent of the Germans in Yugoslavia, others in the machinery of the British government had a hidden agenda. At SOE's Cairo GHQ James Klugmann, a British communist and SOE officer, had been working to undermine the Četniks and promote the Partisans.

Deakin's reports caught Churchill's imagination and he decided to dispatch a more senior Mission to Tito, 'to find out who was killing the most Germans and suggest means by which we could help them to kill more.'[50] At this stage of the war Churchill, the arch conservative, was prepared to find common cause with communists if it hastened Hitler's defeat, even if it implied abandoning his natural allies, the royalists. In summer 1943 Brigadier Fitzroy Maclean joined Tito's headquarters as Churchill's personal 'ambassador-soldier', also representing America.

Maclean was yet more impressed by Tito and the Partisans than Deakin, and trebled Deakin's estimate of Partisan strength. Throughout the latter part of 1943 both Deakin and Maclean would brief Churchill on the military successes of the Partisans and the shortcomings of the Četniks.

In December a Partisan mission was sent to British GHQ in Cairo by plane. There was still a British Mission with the Četniks, but the tide of opinion was turning in the Partisans' favour.

But Tito was intent, it seems, on keeping his options open. In March 1943 he sent Milovan Djilas, Koča Popović and Vladimir Velebit to Zagreb to discuss prisoner exchanges with the Germans. Among the prisoners whose release they secured was Herta Hass, Tito's wife. According to Milovan Djilas, however, the discussions moved onto the subject of a possible truce, then onto what might happen should the Allies land on the Dalmatian coast, something neither side wanted. Djilas and Velebit told the Germans that if the Allies were to invade in co-operation with the Četniks, the Partisans would attack them.[51] Tito avoided the subject for decades and then, in 1978, claimed that his emissaries had exceeded their orders in discussing anything beyond prisoner exchanges. The three emissaries, by contrast, recall that Tito had given clear instructions on every point they discussed.[52]

Fitzroy Maclean was a tall, lean Scottish aristocrat with a love of adventure, who some believe was Ian Fleming's model for James Bond. During Stalin's purges he was an officer of the secret service in Moscow, witnessing show trials and exploring little-known parts of the USSR. When the war broke out he was not allowed to join the Army or resign from his post in the secret service, so he connived to become an MP, then a soldier. He was a founder member of the Special Air Service (SAS) in North Africa before he reached the Balkans.

Emboldened by his successes against the Germans and increasing British support, on 29 November Tito convened the Second

Tito and Fitzroy Maclean

AVNOJ in the Bosnian fortress town of Jajce, a year after the first meeting in Bihać.

It was an opportune moment to turn towards the future of Yugoslavia. In the wider war the tipping point had come, and the defeat of Germany seemed inevitable, if not imminent. On the Eastern Front the Germans were in retreat after the battle of Stalingrad, the British had driven them out of North Africa and Italy had capitulated.

In a hall hung with a banner nearing the rousing slogan, '*Smrt Fašizmu, Sloboda Narodu!*' (Death to Fascism, Freedom for the People!), delegates from all over Yugoslavia approved the creation a provisional government, the national Committee of Liberation, with Tito as Prime Minister and Minister of Defence. He was also made Marshal of Yugoslavia.

The 'people' of Yugoslavia would have the right to self-determination and ultimately secession from the federal state. This laid the foundations for the 1946 constitution, of which more later.

At the Russians' urging, AVNOJ was almost liberal in its outlook, guaranteeing private property and making no mention of abolishing the monarchy. But there was one great gesture of disobedience to Stalin: the diplomatic line towards the government-in-exile, as demanded by Stalin, was gone. Tito's preparatory signal to Moscow did not have the tone of a deferential minion, but of a confident leader. Perhaps surprisingly for Moscow, Tito sourced his 'empowerment' not with them, but with his own Yugoslav followers:

I beg you to inform the Soviet government as follows: The AVNOJ and Supreme Headquarters of the National Liberation Army and Partisan Detachments of Yugoslavia have empowered me to declare:

First, we acknowledge neither the Yugoslav Government nor the King abroad because for two and a half years they have

supported the enemy collaborator, the traitor Draža Mihailović,
and thus bear full responsibility for this treason to the peoples
of Yugoslavia.

Secondly, we will not allow them to return to Yugoslavia
because this would mean civil war . . . [53]

At first Stalin was furious but, on seeing that the declaration
was not badly received in the West, meekly accepted Tito's *fait
accompli*. The Soviet foreign ministry issued this statement in
December: 'The events in Yugoslavia which have already met with
understanding in Britain and the US are considered by the government of the Soviet Union to be positive facts . . .'[54] The Soviets
also decided to send a military Mission to the Partisans.

At the same time as Tito held the AVNOJ session the Big
Three – Churchill, Roosevelt and Stalin – were planning post-war
Europe at the Teheran Conference. They declared, 'The conference
agreed that the Partisans in Yugoslavia should be supported by
supplies and equipment to the greatest possible extent, and also
by commando operations.' In discussions on the subject, the
Soviet foreign minister Molotov had surprised his British coun-
terpart, Eden, by saying that Moscow was considering sending a
Military Mission to Mihailović. But the decision had been taken:
the Partisans would for the first time receive outside military aid,
and air drops began. More importantly, they had finally received
recognition of their contribution to the war.

If the Germans were weakened, they were still dangerous.
The Seventh Offensive, employing over half-a-million men, was
launched into Bosnia in the winter of 1943–4, but the Partisans
continued to elude encirclement by maintaining a 'broad front',
while striking hard at times of their choosing.

Tito now decided to convert his *de facto* leadership of
Yugoslavia to *de jure* leadership – to seek formal international
recognition. The royalist government-in-exile, however, was

still in London insisting that *it* was the rightful government of Yugoslavia.

On 25 May 1944 – Tito's birthday – the Germans launched a parachute assault on the temporary Partisan and National Liberation council headquarters of Drvar, in western Bosnia. Its aim was to decapitate the movement, naturally including the killing or capture of Tito. When the paratroopers dropped on the town there were no Partisan units in the vicinity, but Tito and Kardelj were both there, living in a cave. Nearby were the British, Soviet and the new American Mission. But, owing to fortunate failures in the landings and the movement of ground reinforcements, Tito, Kardelj, the dog Tigar and the rest of the staff had time to escape through a hole in the roof of the cave and melt into the hills. Once more, Tito had eluded the hounds.

Royal Navy warships at anchor in Vis, Tito's headquarters

After this episode, Tito decided to withdraw his headquarters to the most remote of the Croatian islands, Vis. Although the

Germans held the mainland and many of the islands, the Royal Navy controlled the Adriatic, making Vis relatively secure. First, the new 'Government in Exile' was evacuated by air to Allied-held Italy, where Tito had his first meeting with Churchill. A Foreign Office official's diary reveals how divided was British élite opinion on the subject of Tito: 'Tito was cautious, nervous and sweating a good deal in his absurd Martial's uniform of thick cloth and gold lace . . . The PM pitched into Tito a good deal at the end, and told him we could not tolerate our war material being used against rival Yugoslavs. But Tito must have known there was no real threat against him, since we have consistently done nothing but court him . . .'[55]

Churchill, like Stalin, tried to prod Tito into making some sort of compromise with King Peter's exiled government under the prime minister, Šubašić, but again he was not to be persuaded.

Tito was then taken to Vis on a British destroyer. In the ward-room he allowed himself a few hours of relaxation and refreshment, and despite his halting English, treated the officers to a rendition of Edward Lear's nonsense poem, 'The Owl and the Pussycat'.

Tito was not universally admired by the British. In July 1944 the Catholic writer Evelyn Waugh, at the time a captain, joined the mission to the Partisans along with Churchill's increasingly eccentric and drunken son, Randolph. From the outset Waugh took a violent dislike both to Tito – whom he regarded as a Godless communist thug – and to Fitzroy MacLean. Waugh used Tito's early obscurity to sow the rumour that he was in reality a woman. On their first meeting on Vis Waugh recorded in his diary, 'Tito like lesbian.'[56]

To underline the Allied commitment to Tito, Vis was garrisoned with a brigade of British Commandos tasked with defending the island and conducting raids against the Germans. There were also artillery instructors and a flotilla of torpedo boats and an airfield was built for a squadron of RAF Hurricanes. Meanwhile Churchill had finally broken with Mihailović and his Četniks after they failed to demonstrate any real commitment to fighting the Germans, as requested by London. Whatever fighting capacity the Četniks retained, Tito had thoroughly defeated Mihailović politically.

From Vis Tito commanded increasingly aggressive Partisan operations on the mainland, now with the support of Allied airpower and one Red Army corps offered by Stalin. In September 1944, as the Soviet troops approached Yugoslavia, a joint Partisan-Allied operation codenamed RATWEEK began with the aim of harassing and delaying the German retreat as much as possible. They made a last stand in Belgrade, where on 14 October 1944 the First Proletarian Division working with Soviet armour assaulted the city. The German defenders' position was hopeless, and reinforcements could not break through the cordon of armour around the city, but the fighting went on for a week with heavy losses on all sides.

Tito came to Belgrade a few days after the victory, for the first time since the start of the Partisan campaign in 1941. He reviewed his troops and then told them: *In the most difficult hours of the war, during the most terrible offensives, I always thought to myself, 'in Belgrade we began the uprising; in Belgrade we shall end it in victory!' That great day has now come. Among us there are very few of those who set out in 1941. They built their lives into the foundation of this country that it might be free and what the people wish it to be. Their example was followed by thousands of other. Every rifle that fell to the ground was seized by ten other hands. Glory to the fighters who fell for the liberation of Yugoslavia, for the liberation of her capital, Belgrade!'* [57]

Victory

On 7 May 1945 the Germans in Yugoslavia surrendered. Tito was now the *de facto* leader of Yugoslavia, commander of the Partisan army and head of the Communist Party. No one would order him around.

He had already made this quite clear to both Churchill and Stalin the previous year in one elegant stroke. As Soviet troops approached the borders of Yugoslavia, Tito requested a meeting with Stalin to discuss the endgame. The Russians agreed, but added that he should keep his departure from Vis to Moscow secret from the British. Tito duly 'levanted', as Churchill later put it, from Vis in a Russian-crewed Dakota transport plane. At their first meeting in Naples, Churchill had shown considerable patience with Tito's recalcitrance over King Peter and the Četniks, but this episode infuriated the prime minister, who considered it a deliberate breach of faith. On being dressed-down by the head of the British Mission, Tito replied: *Only recently Mr Churchill went to Quebec to see President Roosevelt, and I only heard of this visit after he had returned. And I was not angry.*[58]

In Moscow, he then tweaked Stalin's nose even more severely. This was his first meeting with the Soviet leader, and his first time in Moscow since the dark days in the Hotel Lux. Now he was no longer an expendable foreign communist cringing in the shadow of the NKVD, but a victorious allied communist leader. Stalin accorded him credit and respect, but expected – as he expected from everyone less powerful than himself – complete submission and obedience. Tito failed spectacularly to provide

Churchill and Tito met for the first time in Naples in 1944. Fitzroy Maclean stands on the far left

this; for Stalin, so used to being surrounded by sycophants in fear of their lives, this must have been an odd experience as much as an infuriating one.

Stalin had never shown much enthusiasm for international communism, and now his priority was to avoid upsetting Roosevelt and Churchill by appearing to be stirring trouble in the Balkans and Central Europe; his disbandment of the Comintern was a signal of this. In the 'naughty' agreement of 1944, Stalin had agreed with Churchill that there would be a 50-50 split between Allied and Soviet influence in Yugoslavia. Should he be seen to undermine this, Stalin feared losing some of the presents promised in the agreement, like 90 per cent influence in Romania.

So he expected Tito to tone down his communist rhetoric and the severity of the revolution in post-war Yugoslavia, to avoid getting into territorial squabbles with the Allies over Trieste

With Germany collapsing during 1944, the Allies started to consider the future shape of Europe. Stalin and Churchill met informally in Moscow in October, and Churchill proposed influence over Balkan countries as follows:

	%
Romania	90 Russia
	10 The others
Greece	90 Great Britain
	(in accord with the USA)
	10 Russia
Yugoslavia	50–50
Hungary	50–50
Bulgaria	75 Russia
	25 The others[60]

Stalin agreed, but later wrangled 80 per cent for Russia in both Bulgaria and Hungary. It was probably a coup for Stalin, which he did not want Tito to imperil by headstrong leadership of Yugoslavia. Churchill suspected that he was party to something not quite honourable and referred to it as the 'naughty document'.

and Fiume, and to reach a compromise with the royalist prime minister, Dr Šubaši´c.

Tito recalled: . . . *the first meeting was very cool. The basic cause, I think, was the telegrams I had sent during the war, especially the one I began with the words, 'If you cannot send us assistance, then at least do not hamper us.'*[59] The Bulgarian communist Dimitrov, addressing him by his old Comintern work name, told him, 'Walter, Walter, the Hozyain [Stalin] was terribly angry with you because of that telegram . . . He stamped with rage.'

Tito went on, with heroic *sang-froid, As I have said, tension arose at this first meeting with Stalin. We were more or less at cross-purposes on all the matters we discussed. I noticed then that Stalin could not bear being contradicted . . . For instance Stalin said to me: 'Walter, be careful, the bourgeoisie in Serbia is very strong!' I answered calmly, 'Comrade Stalin, I do not agree with your view. The bourgeoisie in Serbia is very weak.'*[61]

Tito did not have the opportunity to bait the last of the Big Three, Roosevelt, but he found other ways to underline his new significance in the world. After the fall of Belgrade he moved into Prince Paul's White Palace in Dedijer, and embarked on the

Tito addresses the crowds at a victory parade in Belgrade, 1946

project of regal luxury that would continue for the rest of his life. His uniforms became finer and more weighed down by gilt, his horses were the best and he ate and drank like a king.

On 9 May, two days after the Germans surrendered, so Pavelić's fascist NDH state of Croatia collapsed. Panicked Ustaše, collaborators and their families fled for British-occupied Austria to escape retribution for the regime's crimes. They handed themselves over to the British at Bleiburg on 15 May, but the British then handed them back to the Partisans, a decision that is still the subject of bitter controversy. A bloodbath followed, and as with the Serb death toll at the Ustaše concentration camp in Janesovac, the number killed remains unclear and distorted by propaganda, but most estimates are in the 10,000–25,000 range. Yet more who never made it to Austria were killed in Croatia and Slovenia.

The degree to which Tito personally ordered or controlled the massacres is unclear. Milovan Djilas was close to Tito at the time, yet his recollections are strangely inconclusive: 'Who issued the order for this extermination? Who signed it? I don't know. It is my belief that a written order didn't exist. Given the power structure and the chain of command, no one could have carried out such a major undertaking without approval from the top. An atmosphere of revenge prevailed. The Central Committee did not decide that . . .'[62]

What is clear is that Tito always associated himself very closely with the Partisans. In comparison, in a later age, Slobodan Milošević was indicted by the Hague Tribunal for the Šrebrenica massacre in Bosnia, in which around 7,000 civilians died at the hands of Bosnian Serb forces that Milošević explicity denied influence over. By modern standards, Tito would undoubtedly be a considered war criminal.

Other opponents or perceived opponents of Yugoslavia's new rulers were also treated with great severity. In 1946 Draža Mihailović, the leader of the Četniks, was tried and found guilty on charges of war crimes. His eyes were gouged out before he was shot.

As the new interior minister Aleksander Ranković set up a secret police organisation with the perfectly totalitarian name of OZNa (*Odsek za zaštitu naroda*, Department for Protection of the People). Many thousands of middle class people, royalists, pro-Western people and assorted enemies of the state were arrested and imprisoned, often on the strength of denunciations by a growing network of informers. Tito justified the OZNa as follows: *If the OZNa strikes fear into the bones of those who do not like the new Yugoslavia, that is to the advantage of our people . . . Of course unhealthy criticism, carping, malicious criticism intended to make things out even worse than they are, should be suppressed, but healthy criticism should be valued, for it is of help to us.*

The freedom that the Partisans fought for was of a particular communist brand. Tito won the November 1945 elections by a massive margin, with his supporters taking 96 per cent of seats, but rigging was endemic and barely concealed. Šubašić was given the post of prime minister as a token gesture to the Allies, but in reality his deputy, Tito's ally Vladimir Velebit, held the real power in the ministry.

In 1948 and 1949 34 survivors of Dachau and Buchenwald were tried for collaborating with the Gestapo, and 11 sentenced to death on the grounds that if they had not collaborated, they would be dead.[63] No-one suggested that Tito be arrested for having survived the NKVD terror in the Hotel Lux in the 1930s.

The Serbian Orthodox church was let off relatively lightly, as its autocephalous nature meant that it was easily brought into line, as was the Muslim faith. The Catholic church, with its loyalty to Rome, was a different matter. Evelyn Waugh, who by 1945 was stationed in Dubrovnik, lobbied for Allied support for the Yugoslav Catholics, and wrote a report entitled, 'Church and State in Liberated Croatia'. In conclusion it said Tito's regime, 'threatens to destroy the Catholic Faith in a region where there are now some 500,000 Catholics.'[64]

The Croat Archbishop of Zagreb, Alojzije Stepinac, was among those arrested. He was found guilty of collaboration with the NDH and received a 16-year sentence. In reality, Stepinac had tried unsuccessfully to influence Pavelić to stop killing Serbs, and is now viewed by many as a tragic figure. Djilas, at the time in charge of propaganda and the media, reportedly admitted in private that 'the real problem with Stepinac was not his politics *vis-á-vis* the Ustaše, but his politics *vis-á-vis* the communists themselves, and in particular his fidelity to Rome.'[65]

Following the German surrender there was some uncertainty over the form the new federal Yugoslavia would take, with both Albania and Bulgaria mooted as possible members. In the end the new Yugoslavia founded in 1945 (with its constitution adopted on 31 January 1946) was based on the decisions made at the AVNOJ council in Jajce in 1943. There would be six republics: Serbia, Montenegro, Croatia, Slovenia, Bosnia and Macedonia. In addition there would be two 'autonomous regions': the former Habsburg territory of Vojvodina, in northern Serbia, and Kosovo, which had a large ethnic-Albanian population.

The state was to be based on 'brotherhood and unity', a slogan intended to neutralise the spectre of resurgent nationalism. The experience of the Kingdom of Serbs, Croats and Slovenes and the first Yugoslavia suggested that centrifugal forces in such a state would be strong. The experience of a bitter and brutal intra-Yugoslav conflict in the previous four years potentially made them all the stronger. Some Slovenes and Croats were given to powerful anti-communism and nationalism, while Serbs in those republics and in Bosnia feared the re-emergence of the sort of terror that the Ustaše inflicted on them.

'Brotherhood and unity' essentially meant the deployment of the immense personal political capital Tito had accumulated during the war. Those who were unmoved by this phenomenon were dealt with by the UDBA secret police (successor to the OZNa). The new Yugoslavia, in other words, was a little Soviet Union, paying constitutional lip-service to national aspirations, but in reality prepared to suppress them ruthlessly. AVNOJ laid down, 'the right of every people to self-determination, including the right to secede or unite with other peoples.'

Tito helped to put this provision into context with disarming frankness: *Let me tell those who say the present achievements can still change: nothing can be changed any more. There can be no change because the new federal Yugoslavia has been accepted by the overwhelming majority of all Yugoslav nations. Nothing can be changed because we are all aware that this is an historic necessity.*[66]

As Tim Judah succinctly writes, 'the right to self-determination had already been exercised by the pooling of sovereignty into

Yugoslavia and it could never be exercised again by seceding from it'.[67]

Tito could hardly be expected to say much else while imposing order on a country emerging simultaneously from occupation, civil war and revolution. It might be supposed that he intended to soften this line in calmer times. But by taking his words at face value (as later events would justify), it can be seen that at the foundation of the state in 1945, Tito was laying out the plan for a sclerotic system in which the fractious demands of the Yugoslav nations could only be contained by his own personal prestige. This proved not to be a recipe for long-term stability.

The break with Stalin

Relations with the West and the US cooled off rapidly post-1945 as Churchill's 'iron curtain' fell across Europe from Stettin in the Baltic to Trieste in the Adriatic. Stalin set about ordering what he regarded as his new dominions with patchy regard to his wartime agreements with Churchill.

Tito, too, rejected the continued influence of his wartime allies, the British. Indeed, just as during the war, on this and other points he was more Stalinist than Stalin, and started to become a source of irritation to the Soviet leader at a time when he wanted to placate the West. Tito lobbied Moscow, for example, for a faster conversion of East European countries to doctrinaire communism. What he failed to grasp, or perhaps accept, was that Stalin intended foreign Communists to be vassals, to take orders and not to conduct their own foreign relations, follow radical policies or make 'suggestions' to Moscow. Stalin was much happier with countries like Romania and Poland where communism had been imposed by the Red Army, than with a country that had successfully executed its own revolution, and would therefore be largely beyond Soviet domination.

Domestically, Tito was more of a Stalinist than Stalin. His enthusiasm for imposing collectivisation on the notoriously rebellious peasantry, pursuing industrialisation at breakneck speed and refusal to compromise on doctrine embarrassed Stalin.

Equally, Tito could see that Stalin wanted to control Yugoslavia's foreign and domestic policy and to integrate its economic system into the USSR's through 'joint-stock' companies,

Marshal, leader and war hero: a portrait of Tito in 1945

entirely to the latter's advantage. This operated at the most petty of levels: *As for films, in 1946 {Moscow} imposed on us a block booking contract . . . Thus we got Lawrence Olivier's Hamlet for about two thousand dollars but for Exploits of a Soviet Intelligence Agent we had to pay some twenty thousand dollars.*[68]

Above all Tito's regional ambitions most infuriated Stalin, threatening to undermine the USSR's undertakings at the Treaty of Yalta. Where Stalin wanted docile national leader-bureaucrats who would follow a line devised in Moscow, in Yugoslavia he got a wilful communist zealot bent on regional expansion and Yugoslav interests. In April 1945 Yugoslav troops seized the strategically useful Italian port of Trieste at the head of the Adriatic. Under pressure from Stalin, who was keen not to confront the West openly, Tito was forced to hand Trieste to the British. Nevertheless, Trieste remained a source of tension between Yugoslavia and the West. To the south, Tito wanted to back the EAM/ELAS communist guerrillas against the Greek monarchy and the British, in part in the hope of annexing Greek Macedonia and the port of Salonika, and even asked the USSR to provide material backing.

Even Austria did not escape Yugoslavia's meddling, as Tito believed that British intelligence was protecting remnants of the Ustaše as a potential counter-revolutionary force to be played back into Yugoslavia. In 1946 Yugoslav fighter planes shot down two American military aircraft that were allegedly violating the country's airspace, killing five US airmen. In London and Washington, Tito's escapades were regarded as a cipher for Stalin's policy in the region – the exact opposite of the actual situation.

The greatest sticking point was the notional 'Balkan Federation', supposedly to include the six republics of Yugoslavia, plus Bulgaria and Albania, making eight republics. As early as January 1945 Stalin was aware of Yugoslavia's hopes for the Federation, and counselled caution. Yet in January 1948 Djilas was called to Moscow and told by Stalin, 'You ought to swallow Albania – and the sooner the better.' In the coming months Stalin's line on the Federation oscillated: it was a classic example of bullying by someone in a position of power. He denied Tito a clear path to obedience on a crucial matter, making punishment all but inevitable.

Tito and Milovan Djilas at the Yugoslav Communist Congress in Zagreb 1952

And punishment came on 28 June (an auspicious date in Balkan history) 1948. Following a spring of worsening relations between the two countries, Cominform (the successor to the Comintern) expelled Yugoslavia on the grounds of 'abandoning Marxist theory', slandering the USSR and most intriguing of all, that the OZNa was running a 'disgraceful, purely terrorist Turkish regime.'[69] Other outrageous allegations made during the campaign included, 'The Yugoslav State and Party is full of friends and relatives of the German Quisling and hangman, General Nedić' and, 'the United States ambassador in Belgrade is like the host in Yugoslavia.'

By involving Cominform, Stalin had gone public, and rendered his simmering dispute with Tito a formal breach. Tito was elevated to the level of Trotsky by having an entire branch of heresy named after him: Wladyslaw Gomulka, the General Secretary of the Polish Party, was arrested on the grounds of being a 'Titoist' and a 'national communist'. Senior Hungarian and Romanian communists were executed for the same reason. But most provocatively of all, Stalin insisted that the Cominform resolution of 28 June call on the Yugoslav people to overthrow Tito's regime if it refused to bow to Moscow.

For the Serbs in particular, 28 June is a highly auspicious date. It is known to the Serbs as Vidovdan (equivalent to St Vitus' day), the day of the Slavic warrior- and sun-god Vid. By coincidence, this was also the date of the tragic and heroic Serbian defeat at the Battle of Kosovo Polje in 1389, which in Serbian mythology (although perhaps not in today's historical interpretation) resulted in Ottoman domination of the Balkans. On the same day Archduke Franz Ferdinand was assassinated in Sarajevo in 1918, triggering the First World War. In 1921 the constitution of the Kingdom of Serbs, Croats and Slovenes was declared on this day. In 1989 Milosevic chose the 600th anniversary of the Battle of Kosovo Polje at Gazimestan, the site of the battle, to launch his career as a nationalist demagogue. And with perfect symmetry, the Serbian government transferred him to The Hague on 28 June 2001.

To the Soviets' surprise, rather than being buried in the Politburo, the entire text of the resolution was published the next day in Yugoslavia. Tito was upping the stakes still further. In retrospect he told his biographer, *It was clear to me that the conflict was not a passing affair, but that it marked a conclusive breakdown, a definitive conflict . . . I did not know how the West would react, but I was ready to come to grips with every danger.*[70] As Tito relished his conflict with his wartime enemies, so he relished his confrontation with Stalin as a way to impose his will on his opponents and consolidate his power. He appeared to the people as an immoveable and indestructible champion.

In a very short period the rampantly pro-Soviet propaganda fed to the people of Yugoslavia went into full reverse. This, together with the infiltration efforts of the Soviet intelligence services, presented a problem: might some Yugoslav Party members take Stalin's side, acting as a fifth column inside Yugoslavia? In response to this threat, Ranković's secret police mounted a crackdown on 'Cominformists', 'Stalinists' and people believed to be Russian spies. Even before the 28 June outburst, two of Tito's oldest lieutenants, 'Black' Žujović and Andrea Hebrang, had been arrested for having suspicious contacts with the Soviet embassy.

By the end of 1948 Moscow's anti-Tito rhetoric was accompanied by practical measures. The NKVD tried to foment separatism in the republics, and leaned on some communists to betray Tito. Then came an economic blockade by the USSR and Cominform. Because Yugoslavia had minimal trade with the West, and did not receive Marshall Aid, this had a devastating effect. Worse, knowing how determined Stalin was to crush this first serious outbreak of dissent in the Communist world *pour encourager les autres*, Tito began to fear

Some of the worst excesses of Ranković's terror against supposed 'Cominformists' took place on the Croatian island of Goli Otok. Between 1949 and 1952 over 12,000 people passed through its gates. Many of the inmates were there on the strength of an unsubstantiated denunciation, or, for example, for the crime of listening to Radio Moscow. Prisoners were beaten, degraded and humiliated, although they were not killed. But Tito and his lieutenants claimed not to have known about this. Djilas wrote that he learned, 'the UDBA had devised and applied corrective methods that were possibly the most diabolical in history.'[71]

invasion as, by 1949, Soviet propaganda started to allude to military action, and Red Army units moved closer to Bulgaria's border with Yugoslavia.

Both economically and militarily, it seemed opportune to re-activate wartime contacts with the West if Yugoslavia were to survive. Yugoslavia's anti-Western rhetoric started to soften, and informal channels were opened through men like Fitzroy Maclean and Bill Deakin. The Truman doctrine, which asserted that Communism would bring revolution to one country after another, implied that the West should set up bulwarks against Soviet and Chinese expansionism, and try to split the Communist camp. This favoured Tito, the more so after the outbreak of the Korean War in 1950.

Western countries started to re-arm the Yugoslav National Army (JNA), which was being revamped to face the Soviet threat. The JNA was equipped with surplus Spitfires and RAF instructors, replacing the Red Army advisors who had doubled as NKVD agents. In 1952 Antony Eden visited Belgrade. Tito made overtures to NATO: in 1951 he told the Americans that if the USSR attacked West Germany, Greece or Italy, Yugoslavia would fight on NATO's side. For their part NATO generals discussed the possibility of using nuclear weapons against Cominform countries in response to an attack on Yugoslavia.

In February 1953 Yugoslavia signed a Treaty of Friendship and Co-operation with Greece and Turkey, which in August was formalised as the Balkan Pact, a mutual defence agreement. As Greece and Turkey were both NATO members, the Pact effectively provided partial coverage under the Alliance umbrella. Efforts also stepped up to defuse Yugoslav-Italian tension over Trieste, although this was not finally resolved until October 1954.

On 1 March 1953 Stalin failed to rise at his habitual hour at his dacha near Moscow. When his guards summoned the courage

Old friends: Tito and Churchill in London in 1953

to disturb him unbidden, they found him semi-conscious on the floor, having suffered a stroke. Four days later he died.

Before Stalin's death, Tito had accepted an invitation to make an official visit to London starting on 16 March, where it was intended that the world – and Stalin in particular – would see that Britain and Yugoslavia were allies. Stalin missed Tito's meeting with Churchill (who had returned as prime minister), as well as Eden, the Queen and the Duke of Edinburgh. Tito had made a point during the war of showing the officious Russian Mission that he relied more on the British Mission, which was less overbearing and arranged for far more practical support. After the war Djilas complained to Stalin that Russian troops in Yugoslavia often raped and looted, whereas the British liaison officers never did. The personal connection between Tito and Churchill, Maclean and Deakin had once again become an asset. On his return from London Tito said: *We really knew that we had come to a friendly and allied country . . . We found a common language in all matters . . . We were treated as equals and not with the arrogance we saw in the East.*[72] Washington was also supplying economic aid and political support, further demonstrating to Moscow that an invasion of Yugoslavia would not be treated as a local squabble.

The Ukrainian apparatchik Nikita Khrushchev replaced Stalin. The mere absence of Stalin removed the personal grudge with Tito, but Khrushchev was to follow a less brutal and paranoid course, while purging Stalinists from the Kremlin in order to consolidate his own grip on power. In the space of less than two weeks, by guile, luck and will, Tito had transformed the two great power blocs simultaneously from enemies to cautious friends of Yugoslavia, or at least suitors for her favour.

Why did Stalin seek this confrontation with Tito? There was much about him to threaten Stalin. Yugoslavia alone among the communist countries of the Balkans and Central Europe was not the grateful recipient of liberation by the Red Army, but had expelled the Germans itself. Nor was Tito a grey yes-man of the sort that emerged at the head of other European communist governments. Indeed, his background (if not his character) was remarkably similar to Stalin's. Both came from rural artisan backgrounds in the hinterland of their respective empires, and both had risen to the top of their parties through hazardous underground revolutionary struggle punctuated by spells in prison while the party leadership discussed theory in Vienna or Geneva.

Tito remarked, *The cause of the conflict is simple. The {USSR} had reached stagnation point in its development. The trend towards State capitalism was disenfranchising the workers.* Stalin was too right-wing for Tito. At the same time, years before the true extent of Stalin's crimes became widely accepted, Tito said, *Whoever earns the slightest displeasure of the NKVD is eliminated from the social community. Hundreds of thousands of people have thus been unjustly liquidated. Progress towards socialism has been arrested and the Soviet Union has become an enormous terror state.*[73] In these statements Tito was right about Stalin.

Yet there is something disingenuous here, because Tito did not seek the split, but had it imposed by Stalin. Moreover, Ranković's secret police was imposing its own, much-watered-down political terror on Yugoslavia. Milovan Djilas wrote: 'Josip Broz supported Stalin and Stalin's monolithic policies – in short Stalin's Soviet Union – long before his arrival in the USSR in 1935 . . . Stalin and Stalinism were compatible with Tito's mentality and with the extent of his ideological development. He himself energetically purged his own party . . . I remember Tito and Edvard Kardelj (as former 'Muscovites' they had known most of the Yugoslavs arrested in the Soviet Union) saying the Soviet authorities had relieved us of the burden of "factionalism." How grotesque it is today to hear Stane Dolanc and other younger men in Tito's entourage attempting to prove that even before the war, and right in the middle of Moscow, Tito had already begun his struggle against Stalin and Stalinism!'[74]

Did Stalin fear the existence of an equal? The expulsion of Yugoslavia from Cominform and the subsequent blockade had the effect of formalising Tito's independent path and set up an alternate pole in European communism. If Stalin believed that a few months standing in the corner would curb Tito's assertive tendency, he had miscalculated. That Tito himself felt at the very least Stalin's equal can be seen in the following letter, found after Stalin's death in the writing table at his dacha: *Stalin: stop sending people to kill me. We've already captured five of them, one of them with a bomb and another with a rifle. If you don't stop sending killers, I'll send one to Moscow and I won't have to send a second.*[75]

A belief persists among some in former Yugoslavia that Tito was not a Croat-Slovene from Kumrovec, but a Soviet-Russian imposter using that identity. To some ears his strangely accented Serbo-Croat sounded like the words of a Russian who had learned the language. The given name 'Tito' is unknown in Yugoslavia, but is quite common in Ukraine. Others say that Josip Broz was missing a finger, but Tito was not. When the Četnik leader Draža Mihailović first met Tito in the Ravna Gora in 1941, Mihailović, 'scarcely knew what to make of this Communist agitator turned guerrilla leader, whom he half-believed to be a Russian'.[76] Recalling a meeting between the two leaders, the Partisan Sreten Žujović-Crni wrote: 'Mihailović . . . was surprised that Tito spoke with an accent occasionally found in Croatia. This led Draža Mihailović to suspect that Tito was a Russian, a conviction he retained for a long time.' Equally, many Yugoslavs remain convinced that Tito was a CIA agent . . .

As Stalin's biographer Robert Service notes, 'Thus did one gangster write to another. No one else had stood up to Stalin like this; perhaps this is why he kept the note.'

There are numerous stories of NKVD plots against Tito's life, as this note alludes to. According to Colonel Ivan Somrak, a JNA officer who was assigned to Tito's personal guard, the Russians had even tried to infiltrate Tito's entourage during the war. He said, 'In 1952–3, after Stalin said he could easily destroy Tito, we began to suspect there was a Russian agent close to Tito. Tito's valet, Boško Čolić, had been with him all through the war, and had accompanied him to Moscow by air in 1944 [the 'levanting' episode that so infuriated Churchill]. We interviewed him and he confessed that in Moscow he had signed a Russian document supposedly providing for joint protection of Tito and Stalin. Actually it committed him to working for the NKVD. He was court-martialled and jailed as a Cominformist.' It was clear, however, that Čolić had been duped and had not intended to betray Tito. Somrak went on, 'Three years later Jovanka saw a painting of Tito with Čolić and asked him, "who's that?" Tito replied *That's Boško*, then asked me, *what's Boško doing now?* When I told him Boško was in jail, Tito said, *make sure he gets out*. Afterwards Boško wrote a letter explaining his mistake, apologising and asking to meet with Tito. They met and talked for two hours.'[77]

Those suspected of genuine and deliberate betrayal found that forgiveness was not so forthcoming from Tito. The matter was intensely personal for him – according to one source in Belgrade even in his final years he refused to talk to the parents of one of his children's spouse on the grounds that they had been 'Stalinists' in 1948.

Liberalisation?

As the confrontation with the USSR receded, Tito was personally and politically more secure than at any time in his life so far. From his ordinary beginnings in Kumrovec he had endured imprisonment and the terrors of the Hotel Lux, risen to the head of the Yugoslav Communist party, led a successful insurgency against the Axis, created a new revolutionary state and successfully faced down Stalin. From now, assured still of great (although by no means universal) popularity at home, he could play East and West off against one another.

In 1952 he married Jovanka Budisaljević, a servant on his staff who came from a Serbian peasant family. She was such a politically ideal wife that there were rumours that Ranković had engineered the match: Jovanka had been a Partisan and had no known past relations with men. She was, moreover, 32 years younger than Tito. Jovanka initially took well to the role of consort to an international statesman, accompanying him on state visits around the world and receiving foreign heads of state in Belgrade or Tito's palace on the island of Brioni.

Tito's way of life became increasingly lavish. In Belgrade he continued to live officially in the White Palace, but spent much more time in an imposing private house on Užička Street.

In 1949 the Croatian island of Brioni, a couple of miles off the Istrian peninsula, was declared an official residence, and it became his favourite, where he would spend up to six months every year. Vladimir Dedijer paints an idyllic picture of Tito reading alone on the nearby islet of Vanga, 'densely covered with laurel, rosemary

Jovanka Broz. Her youth and glamour were unrivalled, among the wives of Eastern Bloc leaders until the debut of Raisa Gorbachev

and sage, with here and there a fig, lemon or orange tree. The southern shore is level and sandy and the deep blue water is clear as only the Adriatic can be.' He recalls Tito chiding his dog, an old Partisan comrade, for disrupting his target practice: 'Tito lowered his pistol and called to the dog: *Are you mad, do you want to get killed?* Tigar seemed to feel he was in the wrong and hung his head to whimper. Tigar is at Tito's side the whole day long; Tito talks to him, chides him; the dog is offended, ashamed, reconciled, affectionate, but always at Tito's side.'[78]

Not all of his pleasures were so simple. Great tracts of land were signed over to the federal government for Tito to hunt on. Foreign Communist leaders would be treated to bacchanalian weekends of feasting, drinking and hunting at Tito's hunting ground in Karadjordjevo, known as 'diplomatic hunts'. All over Yugoslavia local officials competed to bestow ever more lavish houses on the leader, so that it was not always clear exactly how many houses he had at his disposal.

There was something here of the boy from a modest background who had always sought smart clothes and respectability, as when he spent his wages as a teenage apprentice on suits. The trials of his life and the iconic role he played in forging Yugoslavia were arguable justifications for his increasingly regal habits. Djilas wrote: 'Tito's luxuries were . . . significant as an illustration of how he subjugated the party to himself, and introduced to the party the cult of universal adulation of his personality . . . Pomp was indispensible to him. It satisfied his strong nouveau riche instincts; it also compensated for his ideological deficiency, his inadequate education.'[79]

Signs of a creeping decadence also began to show in Tito's personal appearance and habits. As the post-war years went on the lean revolutionary and Partisan was replaced by a party man with an expanding waistline, pressing at the waistbands of ever more lavish gold-edged uniforms. 'He used a sunlamp regularly to maintain a tan. His hair was dyed, his teeth were false and gleaming white.'[80] Yet he continued to exert a powerful attraction to women, and to indulge it with decreasing regard for Jovanka's sensibilities.

If his appearance became less soldierly, his enthusiasm for the army never dimmed. Along with the secret police and the party, it was part of his troika of power, but there was certainly an affection and enthusiasm for the JNA that went further than the bare mechanics of power. Tito's relationship with the army used to infuriate Jovanka, who in later years would nurture a feud with its officers over access to her husband. According to General Stevan Mirković: 'Tito wore military uniform very often. He was always involved in military details. It was his personal order that promoted officer cadets to their first rank, and his order that promoted colonels to generals. He was signed the basic guidelines for military living, working and training. He often visited military units, and was present during exercises. In December of each year he directed basic military activities for the period to come. All new military equipment was presented for him. All in all Tito knew the army very well and was conscious of its value for the state and government.'[81] His military bodyguards, like his cooks and drivers, recall that he always had time to banter with them and ask after their families, and was continually interested in their welfare.

A raft of economic and political changes seemed to herald further extensions of liberty. The architects of this line were Edvard Kardelj and Moša Pijade. The rhetoric now suggested that the withering away of the state, as laid down by Marx, would occur in the foreseeable future. Kardelj promulgated a theory of 'self-management', supposedly a devolution of economic decision making to the factory floor level and the remedy to the ill of state capitalism that the Yugoslavs had identified in Russia, as well as other measures in theory aimed at diluting central government

The good life. Tito's love of luxury was renowned: he is photographed here in a speedboat off the Island of Brioni

control and replacing compulsion with persuasion. Economic assets were to be 'socially owned' rather than owned by the state. The strengthening of central government, rather than its withering away, was one of Tito's central criticisms of Stalin's USSR. He had told the Sixth Party Congress in 1952 that Stalin had made a *complete betrayal of socialist principals . . . {for} state capitalism and an unprecedented bureaucratic system.* The executive organs were reorganised to mesh better with an economy now supposedly running on the basis of devolved 'self-management'. Yet, as would repeatedly happen during Tito's rule, in practice this meant an increased concentration of power in Belgrade. Rhetoric and reality were a long way out of step.

The Communist Party of Yugoslavia (CPJ) became the less dictatorial-sounding League of Yugoslav Communists (SKJ). The post-war policy of agricultural collectivisation was quietly dropped. It had initially moved at a ferocious pace, with the number of collectives rising from 1,318 to nearly 7,000 in 1949 alone,[82] and was accompanied by Stakhanovite demands for food production, with harsh penalties for farmers who failed to meet them. In 1950 there was a rebellion of 1,000 peasants in the Cazin district of Bosnia, and numerous smaller uprisings elsewhere.

During these upheavals Tito tended to restrict himself to broad statements of policy and ideological direction. He allowed his lieutenants to swim in the waters of ideology and policy, above which he remained aloof. He had never pretended to be a theorist of Marxist-Leninist doctrine, but rather a practical revolutionary. In the pre-war days this had the useful effect of protecting him from ideological splits and, in Moscow, reducing his exposure to the NKVD. He was an effective man opposed to factionalism, following the orthodoxy of the day. As leader of Yugoslavia, this proved equally useful: while Djilas, Kardelj and Pijade debated policy, he was seldom closely associated with it, being a figure almost above government. This allowed him great flexibility, divided potential opposition to him and allowed the sacrifice of scalps should a policy adjustment be needed: power, not policy, was Tito's element. Aside from ideology, Ranković was allowed to carry the political burden of the unpopular secret police super-structure and men such as Svetozar Vukmanović-Tempo allowed a fairly loose rein in economic matters.

This atmosphere allowed Milovan Djilas to push for greater political liberalisation to accompany the ongoing economic liber-alisation. Djilas had dealt with Stalin during his trip to Moscow in 1944, and developed a powerful loathing for the man and what he represented. After the split in 1948, Djilas was able to indulge his anti-Stalin proclivities as head of agitprop.

From November 1953 Djilas started to propose increasingly radical changes to the Yugoslav system in his weekly column in *Borba*. He criticised 'bureaucracy' and the lavish lives of party officials – which many took to be a barely-concealed attack on Tito. The party generally interfered too much in everyday life for self-management to work, he argued, and the UDBa had become an unaccountable monster in the mould of the NKVD. Djilas, in other words, took at face value the split with Stalin, as if it was truly based on ideology rather than contingency, and forgot that his ideological adventures were supposed to occur within implicit boundaries. As Misha Glenny observes: 'Djilas had uncovered an obvious truth (but one which was hard for Yugoslav communists to admit): that Tito had broken with Stalin but not with Stalinism.'[83]

On 5 January 1954 Djilas and his wife Štefica were accosted by UDBA men while watching *Citizen Kane* in a cinema. He was told to go to Kardelj's house, where his old comrades told him that his political career was over. Days later the Central Committee met to determine Djilas's fate on live television, with Tito as master of ceremonies. He was expelled from the Committee; six weeks later he resigned from the party. But it was not the end, as Djilas transformed himself with typically Montenegrin bloodymindedness from oligarch to dissident. In December he wrote his most radical tract yet, suggesting that the Yugoslavia needed a multiparty system, directly threatening Tito's hegemony. This piece was published not in *Borba* but in the *New York Times*.

However deep their bonds, Djilas and gone too far, and Tito would do nothing to protect him from the vengeance of the party apparatchiks whom he had alienated. In January 1954, at a closed trial, he was sentenced to an 18-month suspended jail term, ostensibly for colluding with the foreign press to Yugoslavia's detriment. He was later jailed twice, for a total of nine years. In the USSR Djilas would probably have been shot, but nevertheless his treatment demonstrated Tito's ruthlessness to one of his three closest lieutenants. At their last meeting Tito told Djilas in front of Ranković and Kardelj, *You are a different man*. Like Hal with Falstaff, Tito had utterly renounced his old friend and comrade in the name of political necessity.

Djilas' removal smoothed the path to a fuller rapprochement with the USSR. The new Soviet leader Nikita Khrushchev was

Milovan Djilas (1911–95) came from a proud and belligerent Montenegrin clan. In his autobiography he recalls a raid on a Muslim clan led, among others, by his father. 'The beards of the Muslim religious leaders were torn out and crosses were carved on their foreheads. In one village a group was tied around a haystack with wire and fire set to it . . .'[84] He was a notoriously violent man during the war, by his own admission cutting at least one prisoner's throat. As editor of *Borba* and head of agitprop, he became one of Tito's closest lieutenants, but took his remit as a party intellectual too literally – just as his wartime devotion to revolutionary communism led him to cut throats, so in the post-war period he willingly exposed himself to disgrace and prison for his belief that Tito's monopoly on power needed to be loosened.

intent on making a break with Stalinism, which he amply demonstrated by executing Lavrenti Beria, the head of the NKVD. Djilas believed that, as the leading liberal voice in Belgrade, he had in part been sacrificed as a message to Moscow: whatever happened during the confrontation with Stalin, we are not about to join the West. In the face of hard-line opposition to reconciliation with Yugoslavia in some parts of the Kremlin, Khrushchev made the gesture of visiting Belgrade in May 1955. With his characteristic lack of subtlety, Khrushchev told Tito that relations could resume based on the formula, 'You [eliminate] Djilas, we [eliminate] Beria.'[85]

Whatever Djilas' role, Khrushchev's statement of penitence was impressive. He told Tito publicly: 'We sincerely regret . . . and resolutely sweep aside all bitterness of that period . . . We have thoroughly investigated the materials upon which the grave accusations and insults to the leaders of Yugoslavia were based at that time . . . these materials were fabricated by Beria and Abakumov, those contemptible agents of imperialism who had fraudulently wormed their way into the ranks of our party.' Pressure from Tito contributed to Khrushchev's famous revelations of Stalin's crimes in 1956, in which he described Stalin 'artificially' creating conflict with, 'a state and people who had gone through a severe school of fighting for liberty and independence.'[86]

In June 1956 Tito paid a return visit to Moscow which yielded the Moscow Declaration; on the basis of a 'complete voluntariness and equality'[87] between communist governments (but not parties), the rift was largely healed.

But it was events in Hungary four months later that would fleetingly consummate the newly-revived relationship between Belgrade and Moscow. As part of the process of de-Stalinisation, the Kremlin decided that Hungary's notoriously repressive prime minister Mátyás Rákosi was now more of a liability than an asset. In June 1953 he was invited to resign and was replaced by Imre

Tito and Jovanka entertain Leonid Brezhnev and his wife in Belgrade

Nagy, at the time deputy prime minister. Nagy set about improving the 'intolerable conditions characteristic of a police state',[88] ended forced farm collectivisation and declared an amnesty for many of those condemned to jail or other punishments for political crimes. At the same time, Rákosi and his supporters remained a force in the government and the party, creating a power struggle, closely related to parallel struggles in Moscow. In 1955 Nagy was toppled (again at the Kremlin's behest) and replaced with an ally of Rákosi. Yet Nagy had amassed huge popular support during his brief rule, and resentment of his dismissal grew rapidly.

One of the events that caused this resentment to boil over into revolution was directly linked to Tito. In 1948 – the year of the Tito-Stalin split – Stalin had ordered the arrest of senior Jewish communists in the satellite states, probably to sow terror in the hearts of their colleagues and to discredit Tito. In Hungary the victim was the foreign minister, Lászlo Rajk. Under severe torture he admitted, among other things, that Ranković had recruited him to lead a *coup d'état* against Rákosi's government. He was hanged for his supposed crimes.

In 1956 Tito and Hungarian reformists successfully lobbied

for Rajk's posthumous rehabilitation as an innocent victim of Stalin. As he had pressured Khrushchev to reveal the extent of Stalin's paranoid mania, so here Tito was determined to ensure that his version of events – in this case the truth – prevailed. A memorial for Rajk proved to be the release valve for frustration with the regime and domination by Moscow, and it ended in riots, including the toppling of a huge statue of Stalin.

The Hungarians were unlucky, as they have tended to be throughout their history, in that their revolution erupted on the same day as the Suez crisis, splitting the attention of the West. Hungary came off worse, and the Soviets were given effective *carte blanche* to do as they chose.

Tito's public and private attitudes to the Hungarian revolt were initially ambiguous. In public he voiced mild condemnation of the first Red Army incursion into Hungary on 26–28 October. But then Nagy announced that Hungary would leave the Warsaw Pact, causing Khrushchev to fear that a chain reaction would start among the satellite states. On 2 November Krushchev flew to Brioni to canvass Tito's support for a second, decisive military action against the Hungarians. As the tanks moved towards Hungary, Tito and Khrushchev talked until 5am. They discussed who would be the best successor leader for Moscow to impose, according to the Yugoslav ambassador to Moscow, who was present. Ultimately, although Tito did not approve of the USSR invading another communist country, he could see that a reform movement could easily get out of hand and unseat a communist government. His fear of the latter outweighed his disapproval of the former, and Khrushchev received the support he had come for. The next night the tanks rolled into Budapest.

As lightly-armed Hungarian civilians struggled to hold back the Russian tanks, Nagy and some of his supporters sought refuge in the Yugoslav embassy on 4 November. Nagy was on good terms with several Yugoslav diplomats, and might reasonably

The doomed Hungarian prime minister, Imre Nagy, 1956

Imre Nagy (1896–1958), the leader of Hungary's 1956 revolution, was like Tito a veteran communist who had spent many years in the USSR, and had fought in the Spanish Civil War. He represented the reform wing of Hungary's communist party, bringing him into conflict with the Stalinist Mátyás Rákosi. In plotting a course for Hungary less tied to the USSR – but still communist – he might have been a natural ally for Tito. But during the 1956 revolution realpolitik dictated Tito's line, and his direct collusion with Khrushchev's government, leading directly to Nagy's capture and eventual execution. During his secret trial Nagy declined to beg for mercy and instead asserted that he would be judged by Hungarian history, which proved to be the case: Nagy remains a Hungarian national hero and martyr.

have assumed that Tito, who had successfully faced down the USSR himself, would be sympathetic. This was a great miscalculation. János Kádár, the new Khrushchev-Tito approved leader, negotiated safe passage from the embassy for Nagy and immunity from prosecution, which Tito insisted should be put in writing. Minutes after leaving the embassy Nagy was seized by Russian troops (who were not bound by the Hungarian-Yugoslav document on Nagy's safe passage), and was executed in June 1958. This once again strained Yugoslav-Soviet relations.

Tito's opinion after the events was this: . . . *we are opposed to the intervention of foreign military forces. But which was the lesser evil? Chaos, civil war, or an intervention by Soviet troops? . . . I say clearly that the first alternative was the worst thing that could have occurred, and the second, the intervention of Soviet troops, was a necessary evil.*[89] Yet the US government was sufficiently convinced of Tito's opposition to the Soviet invasion that the following year, 1957, marked the high point of US economic aid under the Mutual Security Act.[90]

Yugoslavia was liberalising, but Tito made sure he had a firm grip on both the throttle and more importantly, the brake.

Non-Alignment

By adventure and misadventure as much as by design, by the 1960s Tito's foreign and domestic policies coalesced into a distinctive whole. Marko Vrhunac, Tito's economic advisor, said: 'Tito's policy was based on four elements: national liberation; socialist self-management; federalism and "brotherhood and unity" and; non-alignment in foreign policy.'[91] In each case Yugoslavia was pursuing its own path, something akin to a 'third way' between the communist East and capitalist West. The last element, non-alignment, is perhaps the thing Tito is most famous for outside of Yugoslavia. He travelled so extensively during the 1960s and 1970s that the *Economist* ran a cover story headlined 'Tito the African'.

He was widely regarded as the master of Yugoslavia's foreign policy, preferring it to the home front, which was mired in economic detail, prone to getting bogged down and riddled with risk. Foreign statesmanship was glamorous and offered the chance to play on a world stage. Tito enjoyed international travel, and believed that a global role reinforced his position at home.

Finding a Yugoslav 'path to Socialism' had made few friends in the communist world. Even after the formal reconciliation with the USSR in 1955, relations were far from calm and predictable and Yugoslavia chose to not to join the Warsaw Pact military alliance of European communist states, founded in 1955, and to remain outside the Comecon economic bloc. Both China and Albania excoriated Tito for the crime of 'revisionism'. On the other side, Tito had achieved working relations with the West,

Tito and Jovanka disembark from the yacht *Galeb* on a visit to the Burmese government in Rangoon

and had joined Greece and Turkey in the Balkan Pact, but would not countenance joining NATO.

In one sense Yugoslavia was stuck in the no man's land of the Cold War, but in another it had enviable independence and could receive economic favours from both superpowers while entering the camp of neither. Yet should the USSR attack Yugoslavia as it had done Hungary – or menace it with nuclear attack – there was no guarantee that the West would intervene.

Tito needed a way to increase Yugoslavia's international influence and capitalise on his novel course. And while 'self-management' in the domestic economy offered a way to differentiate Yugoslavia from Soviet 'state capitalism', so a symbol of independent policy was needed in foreign policy.

The answer was non-alignment, both an international movement with Tito as its *de facto* head, and the name given to Tito's foreign policy. But at first Tito had little interest in international diplomacy and did not actively seek the role he later assumed. Janez Stanovnik was Kardelj's personal secretary from 1945 to 1952 and then a diplomat in the UN until 1957. He said, 'most important foreign policy decisions in the post-war period were made around the billiard table in Užice ulica. So the billiard players, not the politburo, were the most influential figures. The first among these was Ranković, followed by Kardelj. Others were occasionally invited, and Djilas was not regularly involved in policymaking. Tito was as a rule not closely involved in foreign policy at that time: even during the Trieste crisis, Kardelj set the line, and Tito provided the rhetoric. He took no real interest in the UN.'[92]

But as the need to gather wider international support became apparent, the UN was the obvious forum to begin the process. During the confrontation with Stalin in 1950 Yugoslavia was a temporary member of the UN Security Council, and voted with the Western powers to defend South Korea from North Korea. Yugoslavia was sending a message that aggression against smaller countries (including by proxy) was something that the UN should oppose by force.

Later in the 1950s a group of Third Wworld countries started to press their interests in the UN, and some were drawn to Yugoslavia as a standard bearer. According to Stanovnik, 'India [under Nehru's leadership] took a friendly attitude to us. They were not socialist, but revealed to Tito that the world was a bit bigger than the Comintern had told him it was, that non-communists like Nehru could have popular and democratic attitudes. He suddenly felt he might have some support to end his isolation.'

Tito's position invited sympathy from many countries in the 'south' as well as India. Initially this took the form of more co-ordinated lobbying in the UN led by Yugoslavia, Burma, Egypt, India and Chile. Their concerns were above all economic, centering on the policies of the IMF and World Bank and the trade situation. Ironically, this created an unspoken accord with the US, which wanted to liberalise world trade and break into markets previously dominated by the old colonial powers.

Stanovnik insists that this process was largely spontaneous: 'Yugoslavia was not of the south, but its position against Stalin and the West aroused the sympathies of the south. It was much more spontaneous than engineered.'

The most tangible result of this in the UN was the creation of the UN Conference on Trade and Development (UNCTAD) in 1964. Usually UN draft resolutions have two or three sponsor states. UNCTAD's draft resolution in 1962 had a massive 77 sponsors from the Third World.

But it was outside the UN that this emerging movement would crystallise. In early 1955, on the eve of reconciliation with Khrushchev's Kremlin, Tito visited Burma, India and Egypt. He established warm relations with the Indian prime minister Jawaharlal Nehru and with Egypt's Gamal Abdel Nasser. The same year the Non-Aligned Movement (NAM) was founded, intended to provide an umbrella for Third World countries that generally leaned left, but did not wish to accept the patronage of either superpower. The next year Tito, Nasser and Nehru met in Brioni and signed the 'Brioni Declaration' on the NAM. By hosting the meeting, Tito made clear his intention to dominate and guide the movement.

But it was not until 1961, when Tito held the organisation's first summit in Belgrade, that the movement gathered any real momentum. Leaders of 25 states came to Belgrade and Tito was one of the five founders along with Nehru, Nasser, Sukarno of Indonesia and Nkrumah of Ghana. In Yugoslavia's case, non-alignment was promulgated for the first time as an official policy.

As the most developed of the bloc, and with a charismatic president in the shape of Tito, Yugoslavia became the *de facto* leader of the NAM.

But the creation of the NAM caused some dissonance in Tito's Moscow-trained mind. While the conference was being planned he consulted Stanovnik: 'The main issue troubling him was how these people who had previously lived under colonialism and who had no knowledge of Marxism could be sympathetic to us. If they were so dependent on foreign trade, how could they dare to oppose the colonial powers and take an independent view?'

Yugoslavia in the NAM was supposedly 'non-aligned', but it was certainly not neutral in the ideological and military sense of Austria, Sweden, Finland and Switzerland. The Third World bloc Tito assumed moral leadership of mostly attributed their woes to the legacy of Western imperialism. In alleging that neo-colonialist economic domination of the Third World had replaced direct

The leading lights of the Non-Aligned Movement: Nasser, Nehru and Tito

colonial rule, the NAM was a direct predecessor of the contemporary anti-globalisation movement, and explicitly anti-Western. Tito's New International Economic Order plan envisaged huge transfers of resources from Western countries to the Third World.

The NAM was also far closer to the USSR than its name suggested. Although Khrushchev and Tito's relations had soured after the execution of Imre Nagy, Khrushchev valued the access Yugoslavia could provide to wavering members of the movement, and approved of the generally anti-capitalist tone of the organisation's rhetoric. Yugoslav diplomats in Egypt, and Algeria reportedly opened doors for Soviet 'advisors' and arms supplies.[93]

Among the founders of the movement Tito particularly esteemed Nehru, but his closest relationship was with Nasser. According to Tito's bodyguard, 'They were very friendly together. Whenever Nasser had a problem he came to see Tito, often informally and in secret.'[94] Nasser regarded Tito as something akin to a guru, and kept his photograph on his desk. Palestine, in the shape of Yasser Arafat's Palestinian Liberation Organisation (PLO) was also a member, and together with Nasser helped to propel the NAM and Yugoslavia in an anti-Western and anti-Israeli direction.

In 1967, as Israel faced Arab armies massing on its borders (mostly armed by Yugoslavia and the USSR), the Jewish state made a pre-emptive attack. In the ensuing Six Day War the Arabs relied heavily on huge airlifts of Soviet military equipment and ammunition. Tito granted Soviet military aircraft overflight and refuelling facilities for the first time, and went on to do so on many occasions,[95] as it was also to allow Soviet naval vessels to dock and re-supply. During and immediately after the conflict Tito twice attended ministerial meetings of the Warsaw Pact. No record remains of his contribution, but this was not the action of a neutral leader.

This conversion to the Arab cause was a *volte face* for Tito. Pre-war Yugoslavia had significant Jewish enclaves, and Jews provided some outstanding members of the Yugoslav communist movement, most famously own Tito's intellectual mentor and cellmate Moša Pijade. During the war many Jews fought as Partisans, and several prominent Israeli generals were former Yugoslav Partisans. These links, together with the perception of Israel as a 'progressive' state, generated huge sympathy for Israel in Yugoslavia, and naturally Yugoslavia was a sponsor for the recognition of Israel in the UN in 1948. And yet Tito's diplomatic and intelligence contacts with Israel continued at a discreet level – in the microcosm of the Middle East, Tito was again playing both sides for maximum influence.

The Soviet invasion of Prague in 1968 (the 'Prague Spring', more fully covered later) presented a thorny question. Tito condemned the invasion in strong terms, comparing it to Stalin's threats against Yugoslavia in 1948, and the Yugoslav press whipped up fears of a Soviet invasion. Yet again, however, the breach was short-lived, and within a year Tito and Leonid Brezhnev, the Soviet leader, were making conciliatory noises to each other. Again in 1973 Tito strongly backed the Arab-Soviet side in the Yom Kippur War. In the mid-1970s Tito told a group of Czech military officers: *We are not formally members of the Warsaw Pact. But if the cause of socialism, communism and the working class, should be endangered, we shall know where we stand. We hold our aims in common with the Soviet Union.*[96]

While the NAM sometimes irritated Washington, it did not change the basic policy of supporting Yugoslavia to keep it out of the Soviet camp. US diplomats believed that Yugoslavia under Tito was inevitably preferable to a fully Sovietised Yugoslavia, and should therefore receive aid as long as it remained outside the Warsaw Pact. Around 500,000 Yugoslav émigrés in the US campaigned for this aid to cease. Their champion in Washington, Senator William Proxmire, wrote that the NAM was Tito's own pro-Soviet vehicle, 'Proselytising the newly emerging countries of Asia and Africa in what he [Tito] calls international proletarianism.'[97]

Yet by the late 1970s Yugoslavia's position in the radical vanguard of the movement had waned. Cuba, Vietnam and Libya were working to convert it into a nakedly pro-Soviet organisation. In August 1979, aged 87, Tito attended the sixth conference of the NAM in Havana, the capital of the most obvious Soviet client in the movement. Fidel Castro proposed two motions that obviously served Moscow's interests in Cambodia and Egypt, and which raised fears among some of Soviet interference in their own affairs. Tito's uncompromising opposition to the Soviet invasion of Afghanistan later that year showed that however anti-Western his ideological posturings, the spirit of the struggle with Stalin persisted: no-one, including the Soviet Union, would be allowed to threaten Yugoslavia.

Ultimately the NAM was of little consequence to the world and of little practical value to Yugoslavia. It did not adhere to any

Nicolae Ceauşescu (right) on a visit to Paris

properly defined ideology, and tolerated regimes such as Robert Mugabe's in Zimbabwe and the terrorist activities of the PLO. Although it espoused the security of small states, it had no practical military capacity, thus condemning Yugoslavia to continued relatively high rates of military spending. Leadership of the NAM did bring some trade benefits. In particular Yugoslav contractors secured work around the Third World building basic infrastructure and military facilities. But in the wider picture Yugoslavia's exports to Third World countries never passed the level of 26.8 per cent of overall exports, always trailing third behind trade with Comecon and the West.

Nicolae Ceauşescu (1918–89), the ruler of Romania from 1968, was in some superficial ways like Tito, leading a communist state that rejected domination by Moscow. After liberalising early in his rule, Ceauşescu became obsessed with rapid industrialisation and early payment of international debts. Romania became a byword for misery and irrational leadership, with the Securitate secret police brutally repressing the population. Ceauşescu and his hated wife Elena were summarily executed on Christmas Day, 1989, as their regime disintegrated. There were few mourners.

What the NAM excelled in was the production of idealistic rhetoric, with Tito himself in the lead role condemning nuclear weapons or global trade while Yugoslavia's economic situation, political system and federal system headed for the rocks. Again pre-figuring the contemporary anti-globalisation movement, he said in 1979, *The developing countries have no need for so-called aid, through which they are generally provided with an insignificant part of what is being taken away from them under the present system of international relations. This is why this superannuated system must, once and for all, be changed in favour of the New International Economic Order, including a thorough reform of international credit and monetary institutions . . .* [98] Ironically, Yugoslavia was itself distributing aid to the Third World, which it was only able to do thanks to far larger loans from the West.

The Fall of Ranković

Tito faced a dilemma in the early 1960s: whether to loosen the shackles of state control further, or to tighten them, in order to stimulate the economy and counter the centrifugal tendencies of Croatia in particular. Because communist systems had no rational mechanism for change, such decisions often emerged not by consensus or the striking of a deal, but by some greater or lesser purge of the losing side. In this way Tito signalled that the shackles would be loosened, by dismissing Ranković.

A growing economic malaise meant that the debate on state control between reformists versus hardliners was anything but academic, and that clear leadership was needed. In 1964 inflation hit 10 per cent, its highest-ever level, and the import surplus doubled over 1963. Large numbers of people were moving from the country to the town, and needed employment: between 1960 and 1970 a full 10 per cent of the population moved to the towns, bringing the urban share of the population to 60 per cent. Regional imbalances were severe, with Kosovo being among Europe's most backward areas, for example, while Slovenia approached West European standards. Unemployment was being disguised by the growing number of *gastarbeiter* in Western Europe, whose numbers reached 700,000 by 1970.[99] Equally, economic cracks were being papered over with massive and in the long term, unsustainable, infusions of Western lending. That lending itself might be endangered if there were not more sign of economic reform.

In response many (especially Croat and Slovene leaders) pushed for more rapid political and economic liberalisation. They wanted self-management to evolve into a more market-oriented system to improve international competitiveness, and to be freed from Belgrade's economic diktats. In 1963 these reformers got a new constitution, with greater decentralisation.

Tito backed this relatively liberal constitution, but his commitment to reform was erratic, and during the early 1960s he swung between the two poles. He might well act in such an opaque way, for his unique position was becoming still more regal and less accountable. The 1963 constitution brought 'rotation' for all elected posts, which effectively prevented politicians from developing a rival powerbase to Tito's. His position was for life in all but name, and explicitly without other limits. Like a king, his face adorned banknotes.

Now in his 70s, Tito's physical strength was waning. He suffered from sciatica, liver problems, a bad heart, obesity and failing eyesight caused by his massive smoking habit. As he weakened, his tendency to rise above the daily matters of state became more pronounced. He retained complete control of foreign diplomacy and Yugoslavia's role in the Non-Aligned Movement, keeping up a crowded programme of visits and entertaining foreign leaders and monarchs at Brioni. But the running of Yugoslavia fell increasingly to his two most trusted comrades, the theoretician Edvard Kardelj and the secret policeman Aleksander Ranković.

This was not an ideal situation, as the two men held opposing views on reform and both viewed themselves as suitable successors to Tito, breeding a growing rivalry. On the surface, Ranković had the upper hand. In 1963 Tito made him vice-president, the *de facto* heir apparent, much to the chagrin of Kardelj. This post meant that Ranković ceased to be interior minister and formally responsible for state security (UDBA, renamed SDB in 1954), but his influence in practice remained great. He also was Organisational Secretary of the League of Communists, a position carrying great influence. Ranković used this accumulation of power to act as a dragging anchor on both political and economic reform, blocking or sabotaging liberal measures wherever he could.

In any one-party state the secret police is inevitably extremely powerful, running secret and unaccountable networks in other areas of government, gathering information on millions of people and collecting compromising material. Whereas in theory the security service of a democracy works to protect national security, in a communist country it becomes a secret cult of power, becoming a state-within-a-state and a monopolist of the truth. The leader relies on his secret police, but fears it, and creates rival organisations to spy on each other. The fate of many communist secret police chiefs was to end up in their own cellars, or in front of their own firing squads.

Yugoslavia's state security was relatively restrained compared to the NKVD or Romania's Securitate, using arrest and torture much more sparingly, but its leader was not immune to cravings for power. Some observers believe that Ranković, a Serbian son of a tailor, was a Serb nationalist who sought a monopoly of power for Belgrade. Probably this is wrong – he sought power for Belgrade in order to solidify the central control of Yugoslavia, which ultimately accrued power to himself. He would have acted the same way had Zagreb been the capital of Yugoslavia. The point was central control or 'unitarism'.

Tourism was a major point of contention. Milka Kufrin, a former Partisan who was minister of tourism for Croatia, pushed throughout the early 1960s to further ease visa regulations for Westerners in order to stimulate tourism. Ranković was suspicious on the grounds that opening the borders further to foreigners would bring spies into Yugoslavia. Equally, a surge in tourism receipts in Croatia and Slovenia would strengthen those republics' case for greater decentralisation in economic and ultimately political matters.

At first Kufrin found her way blocked politically by Ranković, but then he started to intimidate her. In 1964 Ranković informed her that she was accused of working in the interests of enemy intelligence services and, risibly, of making compromising sexual advances to her chauffeur. He denied her any recourse against the allegations and insisted she continue her work.

Eventually Kufrin managed to secure support from Tito, which, once known in party circles, was enough to remove suspicions about Kufrin and was an implicit rebuke to Ranković. The growth in tourism that resulted from Kufrin's measures provided much-needed foreign exchange and did much to alleviate Yugoslavia's economic problems. The relaxing of visa rules also brought reciprocal measures from many countries, expanding Yugoslavs' freedom to travel.

In February 1966 at the Third Plenum of the Central Committee Tito delivered a speech of remarkable opacity that nevertheless signalled to the party that something serious was amiss: *The question is, how has it come to pass that the development of*

Tito and Aleksander Ranković go out hunting in winter

*Socialism in our country is being rendered impossible. This has been the aim
of the class enemy . . . certain Communists, or more accurately certain members of the LCY are falling under the influence of petty bourgeois ideology
from the West and of reactionaries inside the country who have remained
from before the war.*[100] However obscure the rhetoric, the allusion to
'development' being stymied pointed to Ranković's downfall.

While Tito was doubtless becoming convinced that Ranković's
quasi-Stalinist way was the wrong one for Yugoslavia, he also
could not help but notice that a rival centre of power was developing. Rumours circulated that state security had ears in all of
the senior leaders' homes, including even Tito's. Tito personally
ordered the military counter-intelligence organisation (KOS) to
investigate whether state security had exceeded its remit, a task
KOS set about with glee.

The results were sensational. In June the KOS investigators
reported that state security had bugged Tito's own telephone. A
commission was convened to further investigate the KOS find-
ings, which found that state security's surveillance of both the
general population and senior leaders was excessive, and that the
telephone in Tito's residence had indeed been bugged.

Tito's military bodyguard Ivan Somrak recalls how the state
security bugs found their way into Tito's residences: 'In early
1966 people from the technical department of the interior
ministry told us that they would be changing the phone cabling
in Brioni and the White Palace. We discussed it with Tito and he
agreed. They also sent him two new phones for his office, but he
didn't want them, so instead they were installed in his bedroom.
It turned out the phones contained microphones to transmit conversations in the room. They were not intended for the bedroom,
but that's where they ended up.'[101]

All allegations against Milka Kufrin were shown to have been
deliberately fabricated. It also transpired that Ranković had been
controlling access to Tito and that he essentially controlled the

diplomatic service. State security was found to be running mafia-style black-market smuggling rackets and casinos for the personal profit of its officers.

Details of state security activities in the Serbian autonomous province of Kosovo, which had been quietly ignored in the past, also received a wider airing. Kosovo had long been a source of ethnically-inspired bitterness and occasional violence. The region was considered by most Serbs to be the cradle of their nation and its church, but the ethnic-Albanian population of around 1.2m now massively outnumbered ethnic Serbs, who numbered around 260,000. In some respects Tito's rule was benign, granting recognition to the Albanian language, unlike the first Yugoslavia. But in several other ways the Kosovo Albanians believed they had a raw deal, most obviously in the failure to grant them a republic when tiny Montenegro with a population of 370,000 was a full republic. The inordinate predominance of Serbs in government bodies in Kosovo – particularly in state security – also ranked with Albanians. Ranković had made the most of his opportunities in Kosovo, maintaining massive surveillance of the population and conducting intrusive and inflammatory weapons searches on a province-wide scale. The terror claimed numerous Albanian lives and helped to entrench the feud between the two peoples, a policy which hardly accorded with 'brotherhood and unity'.

The year after Ranković's dismissal Tito visited Kosovo and said, *One cannot talk about equal rights while Serbs are given preference in the factories . . . and Albanians are rejected although they have the same or better qualifications.* A series of small concessions to ethnic-Albanian sensibilities followed.

As a result of all of this, Ranković along with the interior minister and several others were expelled from the League of Communists and deprived of all official positions, but no criminal action was taken. He was finished in public life and retired to private obscurity.

Ranković had been one of Tito's three closest lieutentants, part of the personal cadre that Comintern had advised him to build. In 1941 the dramatic rescue of Ranković from the Gestapo had been one of the opening resistance acts of the Partisans. Having lured him into a trap, the Gestapo beat Ranković unconscious and left him to recover in a Belgrade hospital before further torture and probable execution. Fitzroy Maclean wrote: 'On learning of his arrest, Tito had at once given orders that he must at all costs be rescued . . . barely thirty-six hours after his capture, the hospital was unobtrusively surrounded by forty nondescript-looking men, all Partisans, all armed with revolvers and hand grenades.'[102] Several men bluffed their way into the hospital, found Ranković and spirited him over the wall while a detachment held the Germans at bay.

He had done Tito's dirty work throughout the war, had organised the terror against the 'Cominformists' during the break with Stalin, and had dutifully suppressed opposition for over 20 years. Ranković once remarked, 'If the old man needs to have some ideological problem explained, he calls in Kardelj. But whenever he needs someone to get his hands dirty, it's always, "Go on Marko! Off you go!"'[103]

Where necessity dictated, Tito was prepared to act decisively and without sentiment, although with far less ruthlessness than the Russians. Khrushchev had no hesitation in executing Beria, Ranković's opposite number in the NKVD. Of the three sons, each of whom had the potential to be a successor to Tito, both Ranković and Djilas had been disgraced, and only Kardelj remained.

The episode had two important effects on Yugoslav politics. First, it dismayed nascent Serb nationalists who fancifully imagined that Ranković was one of their number, rather than a Stalinist centraliser. They saw him as a defender of Serbia's dominant position in the federation, a guarantor against resurgent Croatian fascism and Albanian separatism. These festering resentments would grow until Tito's death and beyond, eventually unravelling Yugoslavia.

But the second, more immediate effect was to remove the main obstacle to further liberalisation. By doing so Tito gave his tacit assent to accelerated reform, and found a convenient scapegoat for its slow progress until that point. Marko Vrhunac, a reformist economist, was made Tito's economic advisor in 1967. He said: 'Ranković had monopolised the flow of information to Tito, and so when I came to Tito my first duty was to propose a new system of information. I proposed that he would be informed of everything objectively and in a timely fashion, but only the essentials, on a single sheet of paper, with supporting appendices if necessary.'[104]

Thus Tito tried to wrest back more direct control of Yugoslavia. Conciseness was important for a man in his mid-70s who was president of the SFRY, leader of the party and commander of the JNA. His time was severely limited and he could not descend into the minutiae of policy. He received, for example, about 25,000 personal letters per year from Yugoslavs, all of which were read by his cabinet administrative staff and condensed into a monthly digest listing subjects of concern by percentage. (Some important letters, it appears, never reached Tito.) In addition to these burdens, he maintained a punishing schedule of international travel, and insisted on frequent regal visits to various parts of Yugoslavia to get to grips with problems and meet local people and leaders. As ever, Tito was a practical leader and not a theoretician or intellectual.

So in signalling further liberalisation, especially in implementing Kardelj's self-management, Tito could indicate only the direction and tempo. According to Vrhunac: 'Tito did not intervene in economic policy. He was a communist and underlined this at every moment but he also had a great privilege – he was not dogmatic. Marxist theory was never the core of his policy, he was too practical for that, too involved in concrete life for philosophy or dogma.'

Yet the reforms that followed Ranković's disgrace were hardly radical. Rather than moving further towards the market, as many Croats and Slovenes wanted, the reform mainly took the shape of a redistribution of bureaucratic power from Belgrade to the republics in order to assuage regional economic disquiet and rivalry. Politically, little changed. While Ranković's excesses ended, the reality of a one-party, authoritarian state unwilling to give up its monopoly of power remained.

Structural cracks

In the late 1960s in Yugoslavia, a generation that did not recall the war was coming to maturity: these young adults would not automatically be receptive to the ideology and myth of the Tito cult, while the dismissal of Ranković unleashed a willingness to challenge symbols and institutions their parents considered. At the same time, they saw an international climate that was equally iconoclastic, as 1968 brought turmoil around the world with students rioting in Paris and anti-Vietnam demonstrations sweeping the US.

In these years the policy of liberalisation that followed the fall of Ranković assumed its own momentum, spilling over into student discontent, demands for greater economic liberalisation and for further political, economic and cultural autonomy in the republics, or from some quarters, the reverse. Added to this was a sense of indirection and decline, manifest in widespread corruption and alienation. Tito was obliged to use all of his prestige and guile stay on top of this unco-ordinated unrest from numerous different quarters that threatened to unravel the state and its system.

The spirit of rebellion came to Belgrade in May 1968. Under the influence of some of their professors, students demanded better living conditions and then extended their complaints beyond the campus. There was talk of a 'new left' and the students openly mocked the bourgeois pretensions of the party élite (and by implication, Tito himself). These were not liberal demonstrations, however. Their implicit message was hardline, unitarist and anti-self management, echoing Maoist China's criticisms of Tito.

Several of the professors who inspired the unrest went on to be prominent supporters of Slobodan Milošević in the 1990s.

From whatever quarter, such defiance was not to be tolerated. Clashes between students and police left hundreds injured, causing the students to occupy the university buildings. This was a dangerous standoff for Tito. If it was allowed to continue, the regime's authority would be weakened in the eyes of the population. Yet ending it by force could spread unrest beyond the campus and destroy Yugoslavia's international image.

In a masterstroke, Tito announced on television that he sided with the students, whose demands and complaints were justified, and that the government had erred. Again he was the revolutionary, bringing the fight to the 'red bourgeoisie' in his own autocratic government. He offered to resign if his efforts failed, but asked the students to end their occupation in order to make his task easier. The students were delighted and did as they were asked. Tito had brazenly presented himself as the revolutionary within a decadent government, dissociating himself from failure that a less audacious man would naturally have accepted as his own. Subsequently, much more quietly, instigators of the unrest were arrested and charged.

When Soviet tanks rolled into Czechoslovakia in August 1968, Tito was presented with a further opportunity to bolster his own position and re-unite the country. The 'Prague Spring' reforms of the new Czechoslovak government under Alexander Dubček had aroused considerable enthusiasm in Yugoslavia. In April Tito went to Moscow to see Leonid Brezhnev, who had replaced Khrushchev in 1964, to counsel restraint. In Hungary in 1956 Tito was disturbed by the hanging of secret policemen from lampposts, and shared Khrushchev's view that a counter-revolution was in progress. This time, Tito argued that nothing of the sort was going on in Czechoslovakia, and received reassurance that no invasion was planned. The risk was nevertheless evident, as the

'Brezhnev doctrine' held that USSR was justified in invading other communist countries to ensure the system's survival.

When the invasion came just four months later there was a wave of anti-Soviet sentiment in Yugoslavia, and 300,000 people attended a protest rally in Marx-Engels Square in Belgrade.[105] In public at least, Tito made a partial return to the sprit of 1948, when Stalin threatened to invade Yugoslavia. He said, *the entry of military units into Czechoslovakia, without invitation or consent by the legal government, has given us the cause for deep concern. By this step the sovereignty of a socialist country has been violated and trampled upon and a serious blow inflicted on socialist and progressive forces all over the world.*[106] The regretful justification of the 1956 invasion of Hungary was gone, and in its place was plain denunciation of Soviet actions.

Defence spending spiked and the JNA was reorganised, with a new emphasis on Partisan-like 'territorial defence' forces in each republic, designed to augment the regular army. The people were asked to join this organisation and defend their country from imminent Russian aggression.

Tito's Stalinist instincts co-existed with a fierce independence, and this contradiction provided one of the keys to his complex political character, always mixed with opportunism. So while Tito did perhaps fear that Moscow would deem the post-Ranković reforms 'counter-revolutionary' and threaten military action, there is little doubt that this paroxysm of military preparation was to a large extent intended for domestic consumption. Indeed, there was no sign whatsoever that the USSR was considering aggression, and within a year Tito was again on the path to rapprochement with Brezhnev.

If the episode was designed to focus the energies of fractious Yugoslavs on an external enemy, it was unsuccessful. In November unrest erupted in Kosovo, where Ranković's dismissal had served to awaken Albanian nationalism as much as to quell it. The trouble started when an Albanian student at Priština university found a cockroach in his food and hurled his lunch across the canteen. This sparked wider student demonstrations across the province in which students demanded republic status and some called for union with Albania. The police struck hard, killing one student, and 49 of the demonstrators were subsequently jailed.

With the mailed fist came some concessions. There would be no republic status, but there would be more federal representation, an essentially bureaucratic adjustment that pleased few Albanians. He also allowed the flying of the Albanian eagle flag and gave greater recognition to the Albanian language in the education system, and during the 1970s the local administration was increasingly Albanised.

Along with a new generation of Yugoslavs came a new generation of party leaders in the republics: Marko Nikezić and Latinka Perović in Serbia, Savka Dabčević-Kučar and Mika Tripalo in Croatia, Stane Kavčič in Slovenia and Krsto Crvenkovski in Macedonia. While they were themselves of the wartime generation, they espoused progressive ideas, calling for a looser federation, some political pluralism and greater self-management in the economy. Dabčević-Kučar, Tripalo, Kavčič and Perović in particular enjoyed massive

The hardline Stalinist Enver Hoxha (1908–85) steered his mountainous country into extremes of isolation, poverty and repression during his rule. Religion was completely outlawed and any perceived opponents ruthlessly persecuted. Like Romania's dictator Nicolai Ceauşescu, Hoxha tried to force an agrarian country into the industrial age in a very short period. Hunger resulted. Having fallen out with Khrushchev, Hoxha turned to China, but again relations soured and Albania continued alone, its entire population issued with pillboxes from which to shoot at invaders. Ranković and other hardliners feared that Kosovo's Albanians wanted to unite with Albania, but in reality very few of them seriously wished to leave the communist world's most liveable country for the backward, paranoid and deeply eccentric hermit state that Hoxha had created.

popularity in their respective republics, giving them a legitimacy that the SKJ and the edifice of Yugoslavia was losing in the eyes of many. But their demands essentially required a substantial, voluntary ceding of power by Tito, something that throughout his political career he showed little enthusiasm for. At the same time, fears of a violent dissolution of the federation, combined with the frequent invocation of the Ustaše in Belgrade, aroused unease in many older Yugoslavs.

General dissatisfaction often manifested itself in disguise, attaching itself to an acceptable object, because outright political opposition to Tito and his government was simply illegal. In Slovenia this happened in 1969 over the apparently dry question of road building. Slovenia is a small, mountainous country that had always been the most industrious and developed part of Yugoslavia (indeed, how the almost Scandinavian Slovenia could be in the same state as the severely under-developed Kosovo defies understanding). Since the mid-1960s its people had been able to move freely between the neighbouring market democracies of Italy and Austria, and had seen that a better standard of living was readily achievable. This led to pressure for greater investment in advanced industries, and for more of Slovenia's wealth to be spent in Slovenia rather than redistributed by Belgrade. In 1969 the World Bank issued funds specifically to improve Slovenia's road network. When Belgrade used the funds in other republics, there were widespread demonstrations in Slovenia, and both Tito and Kardelj (himself a Slovene) arranged for a rebuke of the republic's leaders by Slovenes in the federal government.

But Croatia, the second-largest republic, had the potential for much more unruly behaviour. In 1967 Croatian intellectuals had published the *Declaration concerning the Name and Position of the Croatian Literary Language*. This document claimed that Croatian was not a variant of Serbo-Croat, but a distinct language that had effectively been suppressed. This was far from an obscure academic point of linguistics: within the narrow confines of what could be said without inviting a visit from state security, the Croats who signed the document were expressing nationalist sentiment. Tito's response was simple. He rejected the contents of the *Declaration*.

Other Croats were aggrieved by the treatment given to the Catholic Church, by their continued depiction as fascists and by what they viewed as economic injustice in the redistribution of Croatian wealth. Still others simply disliked communism and Tito's autocratic style and wanted to do away with it (although they were careful to clothe their sentiments in language about 'reform'). Tito, the Croat, was a traitor to many of his countrymen.

In 1970, after liberals gained the upper hand in the Croat party's Tenth Plenum with Tito's encouragement, this simmering Croatian discontent boiled over into what became known as the 'Croatian Spring'. Students went on strike and demanded a general strike by the workers. Newspapers started to report real news instead of printing party platitudes. The leadership in Belgrade was at a loss for what to do at first, although Brezhnev had no doubt, and offered Tito military 'assistance' under the 'Brezhnev doctrine'. The offer was politely declined, but Tito revealed it in the hope of alarming the unruly Croats, along with resurrecting memories of the war: *Under the cover of 'national interests' all Hell is assembling . . . It may go as far as counter-revolution . . . In some {Croatian} villages the Serbs, out of fear, are drilling and arming themselves . . . do we want to have 1941 again? . . . Do you realise that if disorders take place others will at once be there?*[107]

Ustaše elements abroad tried to hijack the movement (including by assassinating the Yugoslav ambassador to Stockholm, and by holding a large demonstration in Munich). The Croatian Spring, despite the moderate demands of its majority, was starting to seriously alarm Tito and the Partisan elite that ruled Yugoslavia.

Tito, with the encouragement of Kardelj and the army, decided to crack down.

In December 1971 Tito convened a meeting at his hunting lodge in Karadjordjevo in Serbia. According to Janez Stanovnik, at the time a senior diplomat: 'As at other moments of crisis, Tito brought together 100–150 people he considered influential and deliberated with them. They were not necessarily ministers or members of the central committee, but people he judged to be important leaders.'[108] He demanded the resignation of the three most senior Croat leaders immediately, which they withheld for a week, then supplied. A thousand lesser members were then purged from the Croatian party.

A two-year crackdown by UDBA followed in Croatia, decisively ending the Croatian Spring, in its public form at least. Thousands of Croat students, journalists and others were arrested, charged and jailed. One of those arrested was Franjo Tudjman, who would later lead Croatia in its wars with Serbia and in Bosnia. Some were beaten up or tortured with electric shocks. For example, Ivan Zvonimir Čičak, a leader of the student movement in Zagreb, was jailed for three years for 'counter-revolution', nine months of which was spent in solitary confinement. When he asked the chief jailer if he could be receive some of the dispensations traditionally granted to 'politicals', he was refused and told, 'You people are worse than the common criminals because you put the system in doubt.'[109]

As Stanovnik says, 'Tito was always balancing the republics. After purging the Croats, he had to punish other leaders in the republics so as not to leave them victorious.' Within a year Marko Nikezić and Latinka Perović in Serbia, Stane Kavčić in Slovenia and Krsto Crvenkovski in Macedonia, as well as their senior colleagues, had also been removed. The Serbian purge was at least as significant as Croatia's because it removed the possibility of a liberal Serbian leadership that would willingly re-negotiate Belgrade's relations with the other republics.

The sacking was not a straightforward affair. Latinka Perović, secretary of the Serbian party, recalls: 'They decided that Nikezić and I were the main protagonists, perhaps not without cause. Then they employed typical Stalinist methods. There were whispering campaigns, media attacks, calls within the part for "unity" and "centralism". This lasted for four days, and then we retired from political life. I went back to my doctorate and Nikezić went back to sculpting. Everywhere in eastern Europe there were people who were a kind of bridge for change. That was not present here [after 1972].'[110]

For some Yugoslavs, this marked the last moment when internal reform was possible. By purging co-operative, moderate reformers who had substantial public support and replacing them with pliant bureaucrats and sycophants, Tito squandered the chance to keep Yugoslavia together peacefully, or at least to ensure an amicable separation.

According to Latinka Perović: 'Tito united with the dogmatic forces in the party, which was a mistake. In doing this he prepared the future wars in Yugoslvia . . . Instead of liberalising, he chose centralisation on the basis of the Serbian military and political advantage. The Slovenes, Croats and Macedonians eschewed that, they feared it enormously, and accelerated their integration with one another, in contrast with Serbia, which relied too much on its power and failed to integrate.'

On the economic front, too, reform shifted into reverse. Marko Vrhunac, who was Tito's economic advisor at the time, said: 'Economic liberalisation stopped for one reason; the nationalism in the republics in the early 1970s.' Small enterprises were rolled back and central planning was reinstated.[111]

As genuine reform vanished, Tito offered in its place what appeared to be a package of concessions to the republics in a constitutional amendment, followed by a new constitution in 1974. At the rhetorical level, he was still the arch-enemy of 'unitarism'

(Serb hegemony), and a friend of lively, self-managing republics. In reality they got a constitution that was long on complexity, theory and bureaucracy and short on substance. It was a classic of Kardelj's opaque, dogmatic style. Overlapping chambers, councils and delegations manned by faceless functionaries proliferated at the state and republic level. It was the longest constitution in the world, with 406 articles. Because not even the framers of the document could really understand its Byzantine devolutionary clauses, the net result was that decisions were taken by Tito and Kardelj in Belgrade. The yes-men who had been put into the party leaderships in the republics remained mute.

The non-liberal nature of the 1974 constitution can be seen in the increased role for the JNA. The army was given representation on the central committee of the SKJ equal to the autonomous provinces of Vojvodina and Kosovo: a formal voice in civilian politics. At the same time increasing numbers of generals were appointed to senior political and administrative posts. In public the JNA was extolled as the epitome of Yugoslavism, mixing recruits from all over the country and striving for proportionality in its officer corps. (And failing, as Serbs were disproportionately represented.) But just as important for Tito – probably more important – was its potential to suppress internal unrest, particularly separatism. Tito was remarkably candid on this role for the successor to the Partisans: *Brotherhood and Unity are inseparably linked with our army . . . I believe that our army is still playing such a role today . . . {it} must not merely watch vigilantly over our borders, but also be present inside the country . . . There are those who write that one day our country will disintegrate. Nothing like that will happen because our army ensures that we will continue to move in the direction we have chosen for the socialist construction of our country.*[112] His words proved prophetic, for in the 1990s it was the rump JNA that tried and failed to impose Serbian hegemony over Croatia, Bosnia and Kosovo.

After Brioni, the villa at Lake Bled in north-west Slovenia was one of Tito's favourite residences. It was built, appropriately, on the site of the residence of the Austrian Prince Windisch-Gräz, but the style is entirely of the 1950s. Among the marble-vaulted halls and corridors, the most striking feature is the frieze of the Partisan war, which stretches around three walls of the banqueting hall. On the left it starts with the Nazi air raids on Belgrade, then moves chronologically through the collecting of weapons, sabotaging of trains, fighting in Bosnia, victory over the Germans and finally the bright, socialist future.

Tito realised that he was mortal, but showed a marked reluctance to consider death. He never attended funerals. Yet in his 80s, it was clear that needed both to find a successor and to reduce his workload. One solution would have been a transition to democracy. While this was quite alien to Tito's instincts, there was arguably a valid reason not to hold free elections: it was likely that many people would vote along national rather than party polit-ical lines, exacerbating the already delicate balance between the three leading republics.

Notwithstanding Kardelj, there was no apparent successor with the moral authority and charisma to replace him.

The novel solution Tito hit on in 1970, and formalised in the 1974 constitution, was to rule this turbulent and headstrong country (or, rather, series of countries) by committee. The collective federal presidency comprised representatives from each republic and from Kosovo and Vojvodina. Tito would be president during his lifetime, and after his death the presidency would rotate annually between the republics and autonomous provinces.

The Twilight

Many Yugoslavs look back on the 1970s with great nostalgia. At a day-to-day level most of the country was peaceful and prosperous in its way. Yugoslavs felt pride in their country's liberty and comfort compared to the miserable conditions they knew existed in Romania, for example. Bosnian Muslims – who had received the status of nationality – remember a time of peace and tolerance, and feared the end of Tito. The Yugoslav passport allowed freer travel around the world than most Western countries' citizens enjoyed. Hungarians and Czechs remember how holidays in Yugoslavia allowed them to buy Western pop music that was not available in their own countries; the people of Central and Eastern Europe mostly envied and admired the Yugoslav way, and associated it directly with Tito.

Yet during the benign autocracy of the 1970s, some felt the latter more than the former. Kosovo remained mired in frustration and poverty. Grand projects designed to boost the province's economy had little effect, other than to infuriate Croats and Slovenes who believed that their wealth was being squandered. Around Europe emigré oppositionists – particularly those Serbs deemed 'Četniks' and Croats deemed 'Ustaše'– were hunted down and killed by criminals in the pay of the SDB. Telling a joke about Tito remained punishable by imprisonment all of his life. Croat and Kosovar 'politicals' languished in jail.

Yugoslavia's apparently friendly posture towards the West concealed some disturbing secrets. Tito covertly assisted terrorists such as Carlos 'the Jackal' Ramirez Sanchez, The Red Army

Faction and Abu Nidal (whether this was to undermine Western democracies, or to gain leverage with their intelligence services, is not known). According to Eduardo Rósza-Flores, a Hungarian intelligence officer who chaperoned Carlos the Jackal when in Hungary in the early 1980s, 'Carlos was two or three times in Yugoslavia and rested in Brioni.'[113]

In his book 'Red Horizons', the Romanian defector Ion Pacepa, former head of Ceaușescu's foreign intelligence service, describes the secret co-operation between the two leaders, both of whom enjoyed considerable support from the West. He claims that on a meeting on Tito's yacht off Brioni in the early 1970s Tito proposed a joint espionage programme to steal secret Western military technology in order to strengthen their arms export industries. Pacepa writes that Tito said, *Both of us enjoy privileged positions because of our public attitude towards Moscow. It is at least ten times easier for us to get our hands on Western military secrets than it is for the Soviets.* He went on, *They call it 'Tito's Triangle.' I set up three basic guidelines: Friendly smile towards the West, maximum take from it, and no contamination from capitalism.*[114]

One of the SDB's roving assassins, Zeljko 'Arkan' Raznatović, would go on to be on of the most notorious war criminals of the 1990s, leading the Tigers militia that spread terror in Croatia and Bosnia. Arkan's career as a bank robber led him into jail in Belgium, the Netherlands and Germany. But he managed to escape each time, probably with the help of state security, which valued his willingness to kill enemies of Tito's regime. As the corruption of the Tito era deepened and broadened under Slobodan Milosević, Arkan became one of Serbia's most powerful gangsters and subsequently a militia leader. Thus the unholy alliance of secret police and organised crime that started under Tito provided fertile soil for the emergence of nationalist militias during the wars of the 1990s. Arkan was shot dead in the lobby of the Belgrade Inter-Continental hotel in 2000.

Although not in the Warsaw Pact, Yugoslavia was now

co-operating closely with Moscow. Combat pilots were trained in Russian academies and were forbidden to learn English for fear they would defect in their MiGs. The Yugoslav intelligence services co-operated closely with their Russian counterparts.

After the halt in market reform in the early 1970s, the economy spiralled downwards. The oil crisis of 1973 hit Yugoslavia doubly hard, as many of its *gastarbeiter* in Western Europe were sent home jobless. International borrowing, the oxygen of the economy, was rising to unsustainable limits. The government increasingly relied on foreign debt not only for capital investment, but to fund day-to-day expenditure, and to subside oil imports in order to keep consumer prices stable. Foreign debt reached $5.7bn in 1975 and $15bn by Tito's death in 1980, by which time servicing it accounted for 15 per cent of foreign-currency earnings. Inflation hit 20 per cent in the same year.[115] The economy, like the federal structure of the state, was a Potemkin village.

In this period when Tito's declining personal powers were called on to deal with mounting problems, the splendour of his life and the intensity of his cult of personality reached their zenith. By 1974 Tito had 32 official residences. At the White Palace a special museum was built to house the gifts Tito received from foreign leaders.

Brioni, where he spent up to six months every year, was becoming a second political centre with legions of officials, guards and staff. Tito spent more and more time retreating from his retreat on the adjacent islet of Vanga, where he lived a mock peasant life, rather as Marie Antoinette lived in a cottage in the grounds of Versailles. Here he made wine and picked tangerines, which were distributed to orphanages at new year. A zoo was constructed to house animal gifts. The information plaque in the Brioni zoo today – its denizens now all stuffed – gives a flavour of the kitsch sensibility of the Tito cult: 'Nowadays changed by man, the animal world is not so rich as it used to be and it remains without big animals such as elephant, giraffe, lion and cheetah. Thanks to Tito, these animals have found their home on Brioni'. He is pictured 'bringing water' to a previously arid village in Istria, an almost Christ-like image.

It was here that he would receive heads of state such as Queen Elizabeth II, luminaries of the NAM such as Haile Selassie and Colonel Gadaffi, as well as stars like Sofia Loren, Gina Lollabridgida, Richard Burton and Josephine Baker. Richard Burton had played Tito in the 1972 film of the Partisan breakout on the river Sutjeska, 'The Fifth Offensive' (also sometimes known as 'Sutjeska'), during which he had become fascinated with Tito, and insisted that the screenwriters stick as faithfully as possible to the account in Bill Deakin's *Embattled Mountain*. Elizabeth Taylor was reportedly enchanted by the fact that Tito refused to sign death orders, although clearly this was little more than a

International celebrity. Tito greets Elizabeth Taylor and Richard Burton

formal gesture. In the photos of Tito with these stars in the 1960s and early 1970s, Tito always seems to emit the greatest charisma, dressed in a white safari suit and sunglasses, or walking a leopard on a chain. Fitzroy Maclean remained a friend until Tito's death, spending summers in the house Tito had given him in the old town on the island of Korčula.

Tito evidently took delight in mixing with movie stars just as he revelled in the role of a world statesman; he was every bit as extrovert and theatrical as Richard Burton, and as committed to self-mythologising as Castro. His charming manner, sense of humour and *joie de vivre* meant that people were drawn to him irrespective of ideology or politics: he towered above mediocre apparatchiks such as Khrushchev and Brezhnev, and it is no wonder that Stalin feared Tito's potential to seize the leadership of the communist world. His diplomatic travel schedule remained hectic until his hospitalisation in 1980, and continued unabated even during domestic crises such as the Croatian Spring.

In classic autocratic style, however, Tito's real achievements were not enough, so the mandatory personality cult was added. As well as saving the 'big animals', Tito was acclaimed as an intellectual prodigy. His collected works ran to 24 volumes and scientists pronounced him a genius. Children were conscripted into the front ranks of Tito's adorers. Each year on his birthday the Štafete Mladosti (Baton of Youth) would be carried around the country in relay by teams of children in order to convey their best wishes for Tito's birthday. Until the numbers of godchildren requesting favours got out of hand, Tito automatically became godfather of the tenth-born child in every Yugoslav family.

This pitch of adoration coincided with an increasing role for 'advisors' in the late 1970s, who probably shielded Tito from some aspects of reality, namely the state of the economy and the Yugoslav federation, and the virtual redundancy of the NAM.

In his personal life, too, Tito became more isolated. Since their marriage in 1952 Jovanka had grown into her role as the wife of a world statesman, and was able to entertain foreign leaders with aplomb. At the same time she developed a highhanded manner, a taste for ostentatious luxury and a growing interest in the running of the country. With her furs and beehive hairstyle, Jovanka assumed something of the aspect of a harridan for many Yugoslavs. Tito's bodyguard Ivan Somrak recalls, 'with us guards Jovanka was very correct and polite and never interfered. But she was perhaps a bit rude to the domestic staff. She was in charge of Tito's properties, and so she could be harsh with cooks and maids. The secretaries had problems with her too.'[116] He recalls Jovanka's possessiveness (perhaps not entirely misplaced), when at a party she instructed the guards to prevent an attractive woman from dancing with her husband. Certainly jealousy was part of Jovanka's problem, and various rumours of Tito's infidelities must have reached her, quite possibly contributing to her increasingly unstable behaviour. Her suspicions centred on a woman on Tito's staff, whom she then attempted to remove from her official duties.

Tito's economic advisor Marko

Jovanka Broz's transformation to a harridan and a symbol of her husband's shortcomings placed her in a tradition for Serbian consorts. In 1903 army officers killed King Aleksander Obrenović and his consort Draga by shooting, stabbing and defenestration, largely owing to widespread loathing of Draga. Ten years older than the king, she was unable to produce children, was suspected of harbouring ambitions for her own family and was reputed to have been a prostitute in the past. The main motivation for the army officers who killed them, however, was Aleksander's decision to purge the officer corps – which was widely attributed to Draga. Slobodan Milosević's wife Mira Marković was widely viewed by Serbs as the source of their country's troubles. With her lavish tastes and beehive hairdo, Mira had the classic attributes of a sybilline wife, and she undoubtedly steeled her husband's ambition and ruthlessness.

Tito and Jovanka relaxing on his favourite island, Vanga

Vrhunac said: 'We all treated her as the first lady, she was never neglected. I could see that Tito was in love with her. But he never accepted her attempts to interfere in political affairs. When she tried to do this he was the first to stop her . . . In 1972 when Tito was 80 he proposed to retire step-by-step, but she refused this and told him to stay. This was a source of conflict. Another source was her dispute with the army over his protection. She accused them of abusing their position and trying to isolate Tito. In general no-one performed well enough for her, and me and my staff had big problems. She never knew when to stop.'

Just as Tito's easygoing and solicitous manner kept staff and colleagues in good spirits, so Jovanka's tantrums sowed unease among servants, guards and political staff. In June 1977 Jovanka attempted to prevent the foreign minister Stane Dolanc and the alleged mistress from accompanying Tito on a foreign visit. This was one step too far for Tito, and so he separated from Jovanka, moving out of their house in Užička ulica and into the White Palace. They remained married until the end of Tito's life, and although she visited him during his final illness, there was no reconciliation.

Then, in 1979, Kardelj, the last of Tito's closest wartime lieutenants, died.

Yet Tito certainly saw in general terms the country's predicament. On 2 March 1980 the *Sunday Times* carried an interview with Tito on its front page under the headline, 'The Evening Thoughts of an Embattled Nightingale'.

Speaking in English on the islet of Vanga, he spoke plainly of his fears for the country: *I have given much thought to the future of Yugoslavia. Were it not for my concern for the future, I would not have remained at the head of government until now. I would have retired and come to live here.* He continued: *On occasion I toyed with the idea of relinquishing responsibility to one man, but the choice was too difficult. I had to find a man who had the wisdom to lead the country and the charisma to be accepted by the country. Sometimes I would come across a man who had the wisdom but not the charisma and sometimes I would find the charisma without the wisdom. Finally, I had the idea – based on the principle of collective leadership – to create a presidential council representing all the republics, with the chairmanship rotating regularly between them.*[117]

He clearly saw the dangers of separatism besetting Yugoslavia after his death, as the journalist's notes (unpublished in the *Sunday Times*) reveal: *The wealth of certain republics in any federation is a temptation to the rich to wash their hands of the problems of the poor (such as Montenegro), at which point they begin to look for another future for themselves together with other rich people.*[118]

The *Sunday Times* headline alluded to the widespread knowledge that Tito was in poor health at the age of 87. Ivan Dolničar worked closely with Tito as General Secretary of the presidency of the SFRY and secretary of the defence council in 1974–80 and was in close contact with him during his final illness. He recalls that at his New Year's Eve party at Karadjordjevo in 1979 Tito was in a fairly optimistic mood. In proposing a toast to close colleagues, he said: *There are grave problems for Yugoslavia, but not so great that we cannot overcome them with our combined forces. But we have to deploy more reason on the problem.*[119]

On New Year's Day Tito felt unwell and visited his doctor. The doctors discovered that as a result of diabetes, veins in his left leg were clogging, and decided to operate immediately. The operation was successful, but within days the veins started to clog again and on 20 January his left leg was amputated in Ljubljana. Dolićnar recalls, 'The amputation went well and for a while Tito felt well. We thought he would recover soon and assume power again.'

News of Tito's condition spread around the world, and expectation grew that the 87-year old's life was drawing to a close. During March his condition started to deteriorate again. He suffered fevers and comas as results of a bacterial infection of the liver and the kidneys and by the end of the month was too weak

Tito in his final years

to receive visitors. As doctors in Ljubljana's central hospital struggled to save Tito, a pall settled over Yugoslavia. In Ljubljana a massive security cordon was thrown around the hospital. Only the most urgent emergency cases were admitted, and in the final days doctors delayed pregnant women from giving birth.

On 4 May 1980, three days before his 88th birthday, Tito died of multiple organ failure. Dolničar was tasked with organising the funeral: 'In late March I was instructed to start to prepare for his death. When the doctors reported that the outlook was very bad, we began to prepare for the journey from Belgrade.' The casket was loaded onto Tito's famous blue train and for the journey to Belgrade, stopping en route in Zagreb.

In personal terms, Tito was not a rich man – he had assumed that the assets of the state were his to enjoy, but his salary and personal assets were modest. His sons Žarko and Miša received nothing except for some suits and a few trinkets. Jovanka, however, wanted to retain the privileges of the first lady, and disliked the new political arrangements to boot. She told Tito's *chef de cabinet*: 'Who the hell are these new presidency people?', and said that as his only heir, everything belonged to her. Eventually she settled for the highest pension for a public servant and a large villa.

The funeral on 7 May was massive in scale and pathos. Yugoslavs were excused work and school, enabling mass displays of mourning. Because Tito had been the *de facto* leader of the NAM, and because he was on good terms with both East and West, an unprecedented number of world leaders attended the funeral. They came from 128 countries and included four kings, 31 presidents, 22 prime ministers and 47 foreign ministers. Margaret Thatcher, Prince Philip, Leonid Brezhnev, Helmut Schmidt, Ceauşescu, Saddam Hussein and Indira Gandhi were there. President Carter, however, was not.[120]

How long Yugoslavia would outlive its autocratic founder, no one knew.

Legacy

When Tito died in 1980 he left a country whose economy was failing, which was saddled with unmanageable debt, and with nationalist forces resurgent. Slovenia and Croatia, the richest republics, became increasingly resentful of the redistribution of their wealth. Kosovo, with its Albanian majority demanding greater status in the federation, turned during the 1980s into a sort of Balkan West Bank, in perpetual *intifada*. The 'collective presidency' in its way deepened the tradition of enigmatic leadership Tito had started: it was so enigmatic that few people knew who was in charge.

Many Yugoslavs believe that Tito should have appointed a successor. But as he had told the *Sunday Times*, none of his old lieutenants remained, and no one stood out as having the necessary authority and charisma. Others believe he should have made a transition to democracy in the 1970s. Aside from the incompatibility of democratic elections with Tito's Stalinist instincts, this could have hastened the collapse of Yugoslavia: many people would vote on national lines, and while a Serbian-dominated leadership would have infuriated Croats and Slovenes, a government dominated by smaller republics would have ignited Serb nationalism. Lebanon's system of confessional reservations might have been a solution, where posts like prime minister and president are constitutionally guaranteed to representatives of each confessional group. But the ongoing Lebanese civil war suggested that this had not been an overwhelming success, and in any case the various Lebanese communities live cheek-by-jowl, and could not break away into ethnic-geographic blocks as the Yugoslavs could. Lebanon, in other words, was a slightly more viable state than Yugoslavia.

The rational solution of amicable separation (in which, crucially, Serbia is acquiescent) was briefly possible in the early 1970s until Tito snuffed it out.

Now there was little alternative to the stop-gap collective presidency. As faceless apparatchiks jockeyed for power in the post-Tito vacuum, some turned to the forbidden fruit of nationalism to secure popular appeal.

In 1986 President Ivan Stambolić's protégé Slobodan Milošević became President of the Serbian League of Communists. In the same year he reacted fairly favourably to an open letter from the Serbian Academy of Sciences and Arts (SANU) calling for action to protect Serbs in Kosovo and Croatia. This 'Memorandum' lambasted economic liberalisation, implicitly condemned Yugoslavia and pointed instead towards a greater Serbia incorporating parts of other republics. The document said things that were unsayable in Tito's time, and started to unleash latent and powerful nationalist energy in Serbia.

In 1987 Milošević ousted President Stambolić and revoked the autonomy of Kosovo and Vojvodina. Aside from infuriating the inhabitants of those provinces, it unbalanced the Federal Presidency to give Serbia three votes out of eight – an obvious provocation to Croatia.

Hysterical nationalist rhetoric abounded, and demagogic leaders fell back on mythologizing history. Serb extremists portrayed Croats as 'Ustaše', while Croat rabble-rousers called Serbs 'Četniks'. In Croatia the president Franjo Tudjman was the mirror image of Milošević, and the two in some ways enjoyed a symbiotic relationship.

In May 1991 war broke out between Serbia and Croatia. It was followed by ten days of fighting with Slovenia, which was then

Slobodan Milošević, the President who tipped Tito's Yugoslavia into the abyss of nationalist separatism and internecine warfare

allowed to secede. War then erupted in Bosnia and Hercegovina, ending with the 1995 Dayton Accords. In 1999 the conflict between the Kosovo Liberation Army and Yugoslav forces attracted international attention, followed by a NATO air attack on Serbia, and the creation of a *de facto* international protectorate in Kosovo. Finally, in 2001 there was a small Slav-Albanian ethnic conflict in Macedonia. Tens of thousands died in these conflicts. Eastern Europe's most prosperous state was reduced to penury, and Serbia achieved the status of a pariah.

A Europe supposedly bent on peaceful, co-operative progress not only saw its south-eastern flank descend into a perplexing, apparently Medieval round of internecine warfare, but also found itself impotent in the face of barbarity. At the time of writing the new states of Serbia and Montenegro, Bosnia and Hercegovina, Macedonia, Slovenia and Croatia have emerged from the ruins of Yugoslavia. Yet only the borders and future of the final two seem assured: the first three remain under the shadow of vexing national and territorial questions. For Europe, the spectres of instability and industrial-scale transnational crime are the new incarnation of the eternal 'Balkan question', and a part of Tito's legacy.

Notes

The works referred to most frequently are abbreviated as follows:

TS = Vladimir Dedijer, *Tito Speaks* (Weidenfeld and Nicolson, 1953)
DB = Fitzroy Maclean, *Disputed Barricades* (Jonathan Cape, 1957)
T = Jasper Ridley, *Tito* (Constable and Constable, 1994)

1 *TS* p 3
2 *TS* p 6
3 *TS* p 7
4 *TS* p 10
5 *TS* p 10
6 *TS* p 16
7 *TS* p 19
8 *TS* p 22
9 *TS* p 23
10 *TS* p 24
11 *TS* p 26
12 *TS* p 29
13 *TS* p 32
14 *TS* p 34
15 *TS* p 31
16 K Zilliacus, *Tito of Yugoslavia* (Michael Joseph Ltd, 1952) p 52
17 *TS* p 40
18 *TS* p 50
19 *TS* p 52
20 *TS* p 57
21 *DB* p 28
22 *TS* p 63
23 *TS* p 63
24 *DB* p 32
25 *TS* p 81
26 *TS* p 84
27 *DB* p 33
28 *TS* p 95
29 *TS* p 100
30 Phyllis Auty, *Tito* (Ballantine Books, 1972) p 94
31 Milovan Djilas, *Tito: The Story from Inside* (Weidenfeld & Nicholson, 1981) p 137
32 *TS* p 110
33 *TS* p 124
34 *TS* p 128
35 *TS* p 138
36 *TS* p 145
37 *TS* p 154
38 *TS* p 135
39 Djilas, *Tito* p 25
40 *DB* p 195
41 *DB* p 204
42 *DB* p 209
43 *DB* p 226
44 Fitzroy *Churchill* p 760
61 *TS* p 234
62 Milovan Djilas, *Wartime* p 449
63 Branimir Anzulović, *Heavenly Serbia* (C Hurst & Co, 1999) p 160
64 Michael Davie, *The Diaries of Evelyn Waugh* (Penguin, 1979) p 620
65 Sabrina Ramet, *The Catholic Church in Yugoslavia* (Duke University Press, 1990)
66 Tim Judah, *The Serbs* (Yale/Nota Bene, 2000) p 140
67 Tim Judah, *The Serbs* p 141
68 *TS* p 275
69 Misha Glenny, *The Balkans* (Granta, 1999) p 536
70 *TS* p 390
71 Djilas, *Tito* p 86
72 *DB* p 403
73 *TS*
74 Djilas, *Tito*

75 Robert Service, *Stalin* (Macmillan, 2004) p 592
76 *DB* p 145
77 Interview with author, Novo Mesto, Slovenia, August 2005
78 *TS* p 389
79 Djilas, *Tito* p 96
80 Djilas, *Tito* p 110
81 Interview with Aleks Brkić, Belgrade, Serbia, September 2005
82 Glenny, *The Balkans* p 551
83 Glenny, *The Balkans* p 577
84 Milovan Djilas, *Land Without Justice* (Harcourt, Brace & Company, 1958) p 208
85 Djilas, *Tito* p 165
86 Edvard Kardelj, *Reminiscences* (Blond & Briggs, 1982) p 136
87 John R Lampe, *Yugoslavia as History* (Cambridge University Press, 2000) p 268
88 Paul Lendvai, *The Hungarians* (C Hurst & Co, 2003) p 446
89 *T* p 342
90 Lampe, *Yugoslavia* p 275
91 Interview with author, Lake Bled, Slovenia, August 2005
92 Interview with author, Ljubljana, Slovenia, August 2005
93 Alvin Rubenstein, *Yugoslavia*
94 Interview with author, Novo Mesto, Slovenia, August 2005
95 Nora Beloff, *Tito's Flawed Legacy* (Victor Gollancz, 1985) p 173
96 Beloff, *Tito's Flawed Legacy* p 176
97 George Kennan, *Memoirs 1950-63* (Atlantic, 1972) p 301
98 Beloff, *Tito's Flawed Legacy* p 180
99 William Zimmerman, *Open Borders, Nonalignment and the Political Evolution of Yugoslavia* (Princeton University Press 1987) p 81
100 Duncan Wilson, *Tito's Yugoslavia* (Cambridge University Press, 1997)
101 Interview with author, Novo Mesto, Slovenia, August 2005
102 *DB* p 135
103 Glenny, *The Balkans* p 579
104 Interview with author, Lake Bled, Slovenia, August 2005
105 Beloff, *Tito's Flawed Legacy* p 174
106 Beloff, *Tito's Flawed Legacy* p 174
107 *T* p 395
108 Interview with author, Ljubljana, Slovenia, August 2005
109 Interview with author, Zagreb, Croatia, September 2005
110 Interview with Aleks Brkić, Belgrade, Serbia, September 2005
111 Interview with author, Lake Bled, Slovenia, August 2005
112 James Gow, *The Serbian Project and its Adversaries* (C Hurst & Co, 2003) p 53
113 Interview with author, Szurdopuspoki, September 2005
114 Ion Pacepa, *Red Horizons* (Regnery Gateway, 1987) p 349
115 Viktor Meier, *Yugoslavia, a History of its Demise* (Routledge 1995)
116 Interview with author, Novo Mesto, Slovenia, August 2005
117 *The Sunday Times*, 'The Evening Thoughts of an Embattled Nightingale' (2 March 1980), quoted in *Al-Ahram*, 1999
118 *Al-Ahram*, 1999
119 Interview with author, Re?ica ob Savinji, Slovenia, August 2005
120 *T* pp 19–21

Chronology

Year	Age	Life
1892		Josip Broz born in Kumrovec, Croatia.
1900	8	Starts working on farm while also attending school.
1904	12	Begins full-time cow-herding work.
1907	15	Goes to Sisak to work as a waiter.
1910	18	Works in Zagreb, seeks work in Ljubljana and Trieste.
1911	19	Returns to work in Zagreb, then in Kamnik, Slovenia.
1912	20	Travels in Germany and Austria-Hungary, lives near Vienna with his brother.
1913	21	Conscripted into Austro-Hungarian army, becomes staff sergeant.

Year	History	Culture
1892	Pan-Slav Conference in Cracow. Gladstone becomes British prime minister.	Conan Doyle, *The Adventures of Sherlock Holmes*. Mahler, Symphony No 1
1900	Boer War: relief of Mafeking. Assassination of King Umberto I of Italy.	Freud, *The Interpretation of Dreams*. Chekhov, *Uncle Vanya*.
1904	Russo-Japanese War.	Conrad, *Nostromo*. Puccini, *Madame Butterfly*.
1907	Lenin leaves Russia. Hague Peace Conference.	Kipling wins Nobel Prize for Literature. Lehar, *The Merry Widow*.
1910	Revolt in Albania. Montenegro proclaimed a kingdom.	Forster, *Howard's End*. Matisse, *The Dance*.
1911	Turkish-Italian War. Winston Churchill appointed First Lord of the Admiralty.	D H Lawrence, *The White Peacock*. *Mona Lisa* stolen from the Louvre.
1912	Albania declares independence. First Balkan War: Balkan League takes Macedonia from the Porte. Sinking of the *Titanic*.	Synge, *Playboy of the Western World*. Picasso, *The Violin*.
1913	Second Balkan War: Bulgaria turns on Allies – is defeated.	Mann, *Death in Venice*. First Charlie Chaplin movies.

Year	Age	Life
1914	22	The First World War. Posted to Carpathian front.
1915	23	Wounded and captured by the Russians; recovers in Siberia.
1917	25	In St Petersburg for the July Days. Escapes from the Provisional Government to Omsk.
1919	27	Marries Pelagea Belusova ('Polka') in Omsk.
1920	28	Joins Communist Party in Russia. Returns to Croatia.
1921	29	Moves to Veliko Trojstvo until 1925.
1924	32	Elected to Party district committee.
1925	33	Works in shipyard at Kraljevica, Croatia.
1926	34	Organizes strike in Kraljevica. Works in railway wagon factory in Zagreb.

Year	History	Culture
1914	Assassination of Franz Ferdinand in Sarajevo: outbreak of First World War.	Joyce, *Dubliners*.
1915	The First World War: Gallipoli Campaign. Italy declares war on the Central Powers.	Buchan, *The Thirty-Nine Steps*. Film: *Birth of a Nation*.
1917	Russian Revolution. USA enters the War.	Jung, *Psychology of the Unconscious*.
1919	Treaty of Versailles sets new Balkan borders.	Hardy, *Collected Poems*.
1920	Treaty of Trianon breaks up Habsburg Empire.	Hasek, *The Adventures of The Good Soldier Schwejk*. Film: *The Cabinet of Dr Caligari*.
1921	Constitution of the Kingdom of the Serbs, Croats and Slovenes.	D H Lawrence, *Women in Love*.
1924	Death of Lenin. Britain recognizes USSR.	Noel Coward, *The Vortex*. Forster, *A Passage to India*.
1925	Hindenburg elected president of Germany.	Fitzgerald, *The Great Gatsby*. Film: *Battleship Potemkin*.
1926	The General Strike in Britain. Germany admitted to League of Nations.	Hemingway, *The Sun Also Rises*. Film: *Metropolis*.

Year	Age	Life
1927	35	Appointed Secretary of Zagreb branch of the Metalworkers' Union.
1928	36	Appointed Secretary of Zagreb branch of the Communist Party of Yugoslavia. Jailed in Zagreb.
1934	42	Released from jail. Travels to Vienna to meet Party leadership. Appointed to the Central Committee.
1935	43	Returns to Moscow to work for the Comintern. Also works in Yugoslavia.
1936	44	Divorces Polka and marries Lucia Bauer in Moscow. Returns to Vienna.
1937	45	Becomes Party leader after execution of Milan Gorkić in Moscow.
1938	46	Purge of Yugoslav communists in Moscow: Polka and Lucia Bauer arrested.
1939	47	Outbreak of the Second World War. Follows wait-and-see policy on the war, on Moscow's orders.

Year	History	Culture
1927	Kingdom of Serbs, Croats and Slovenes becomes Yugoslavia. Trotsky expelled from Russian Communist Party.	Virginia Woolf, *To the Lighthouse*. Film: *The Jazz Singer*.
1928	Albania proclaimed kingdom. Croat leader Stjepan Radić assassinated.	D H Lawrence, *Lady Chatterley's Lover*. Waugh, *Decline and Fall*.
1934	Assassination of King Alexsander of Yugoslavia: Prince Paul named regent.	Graves, *I, Claudius*. Film: *The Private Live of Henry VIII*.
1935	Nazis repudiate Treaty of Versailles. First show trials in Moscow.	Greene, *England Made Me*. Film: *Anna Karenina*.
1936	German troops enter the Rhineland. Outbreak of the Spanish Civil War.	Foundation of Penguin Books. Film: *Modern Times*.
1937	Spanish Civil War: bombing of Guernica. British naval agreement with Germany and the USSR.	Sartre, *La Nausée*. Orwell, *The Road to Wigan Pier*.
1938	German-Austrian *anschluss*. The Munich Conference: Germany occupies the Sudetenland.	Du Maurier, *Rebecca*. Film: *Alexander Nevski*.
1939	Nazi-Soviet Pact signed. German invasion of Poland.	Steinbeck, *The Grapes of Wrath*. Film: *Gone with the Wind*.

Year	Age	Life
1940	48	Returns to Moscow: organizes Fifth National Conference underground in Zagreb.
1941	49	Axis invasion of Yugoslavia. Partisan uprising begins in Serbia.
1942	50	Eludes Axis offensives in Bosnia and Montenegro: mounts own offensive into Croatia. First AVONJ.
1943	51	New Axis offensives unsuccessful. British liaison officer joins the Partisans. Second AVONJ.
1944	52	Narrowly escapes German attack on HQ at Drvar: moves to the island of Vis. Belgrade liberated by Partisans and Red Army troops.
1945	53	Germans in Yugoslavia surrender. Visits Moscow. Declares the new Yugoslavia.
1946	54	Wartime enemy Draža Mihailović tried and executed. Yugoslav fighters shoot down US aircraft.
1948	56	Yugoslavia expelled from Cominform.

Year	History	Culture
1940	German *blitzkrieg* in the West: the fall of France. The Battle of Britain.	Chandler, *Farewell My Lovely*. Film: *Fantasia*.
1941	German invasion of USSR. Japanese attack Pearl Harbor: USA enters the war.	Noel Coward, *Blithe Spirit*. Film: *Citizen Kane*.
1942	British victory at El Alamein. US troops land in North Africa.	Camus, *L'Étranger*. Film: *Mrs Miniver*.
1943	Allied invasion of Italy. Mussolini deposed. Germans defeated at Stalingrad. Comintern disbanded.	Film: *Casablanca*.
1944	Allies land in Normandy. Churchill and Stalin agree on 'percentage' of influence in Eastern Europe.	T S Eliot, *Four Quartets*. Film: *Henry V*.
1945	Hitler commits suicide: Germany surrenders. Dropping of two atomic bombs forces Japanese surrender.	Waugh, *Brideshead Revisited* Film: *The Lost Weekend*.
1946	First session of UN General Assembly in London. Churchill's 'Iron Curtain' speech.	Rattigan, *The Winslow Boy*. Film: *La Belle et la Bête*.
1948	State of Israel founded. Marshall Plan begins. The Berlin airlift.	Greene, *The Heart of The Matter*. Film: *The Bicycle Thief*.

Year	Age	Life
1949	57	Goli Otok concentration camp opens – Tito later denies knowledge. Brioni becomes official residence.
1952	60	Marries Jovanka Budisaljević. Anthony Eden visits Belgrade.
1953	61	Becomes President of Yugoslavia. Visits London. Tito signs treaty with NATO members Greece and Turkey.
1954	62	Milovan Djilas arrested. Visits to Greece and India.
1955	63	Brioni Declaration of formation of Non-Aligned Movement (NAM). Receives Khrushchev in Belgrade.
1956	64	Tito visits Moscow. Secret meeting with Khrushchev at Brioni. Soviets invade Hungary.
1961	69	Receives 25 foreign leaders at Belgrade summit of NAM.
1963	71	Approves new constitution with 'rotation' of officials.

Year	History	Culture
1949	NATO founded. Soviets test first atomic bomb. Mao proclaims People's Republic of China.	Orwell, *Nineteen Eighty Four*. Film: *The Third Man*.
1952	Queen Elizabeth II succeeds to the throne. Eisenhower elected US president.	Leavis, *The Common Pursuit*. Film: *High Noon*.
1953	Armistice signed in Korean War. Stalin dies, succeeded by Khrushchev.	Fleming, *Casino Royale*. Film: *Roman Holiday*.
1954	Potomac Charter signed by Eisenhower and Churchill. French defeat at Dien Bien Phu.	Mann, *Felix Krull*. Film: *The Seven Samurai*.
1955	Churchill resigns as Prime Minister. Germany joins NATO.	Greene, *The Quiet American*. Film: *The Seven Year Itch*.
1956	Khrushchev denounces Stalin. Invasion of Suez by British and French.	Osborne, *Look Back in Anger*. Film: *The Ten Commandments*.
1961	President Kennedy inaugurated. Bay of Pigs crisis.	Stone, *The Agony and the Ecstasy*. Film: *West Side Story*.
1963	Assassination of President Kennedy. Castro visits the USSR.	Le Carré, *The Spy Who Came in From the Cold*. Film: *Tom Jones*.

Year	Age	Life
1966	74	Dismisses Aleksander Ranković from vice-presidency.
1967	75	Grants Soviet aircraft overflight and refuelling rights during Six Day War.
1968	76	Criticizes Moscow for invasion of Czechoslovakia. Appears on television to appease student unrest.
1970	78	Elaborates rotating presidency idea.
1971	79	Decides at Karadjordjevo to repress nascent liberal movement. Troops end 'Croatian Spring' – mass arrests follow.
1972	80	Agrees to gradual retirement.
1973	81	Takes Arab side in Yom Kippur War.
1974	82	Approves new constitution supposedly giving more power to republics. Rotating presidency.

Year	History	Culture
1966	British PM Wilson visits Moscow. Ghana's President Nkrumah deposed in coup.	Capote, *In Cold Blood*. Film: *Fahrenheit 451*.
1967	Hanoi attacked by US bombers.	Pinter, *The Homecoming*. Film: *Blow-Up*.
1968	Student disturbances in Paris. Tet Offensive in Vietnam.	Vidal, *Myra Breckenridge*. Film: *2001: A Space Odyssey*.
1970	Biafran forces surrender to Nigeria. Four US student protestors killed at Kent State.	Mortimer, *A Voyage Round My Father*. Film: *Catch-22*.
1971	Vietnam War spreads to Cambodia and Laos. India-Pakistan War.	Plath, *The Bell Jar*. Film: *A Clockwork Orange*.
1972	Nixon visits China and Russia. Coal strike in Britain.	Films: *The Godfather*, *Cabaret*.
1973	US troops withdraw from Vietnam. Watergate.	Film: *Last Tango in Paris*.
1974	Nixon resigns as US President.	Benchley, *Jaws*.

Year	Age	Life
1977	85	Estranged from wife Jovanka.
1979	87	Defies Castro at NAM Conference in Havana. Edvard Kardelj dies.
1980	87	4 May: dies in Ljubljana, one day before his 88th birthday.

Year	History	Culture
1977	Egyptian President Sadat visits Israel.	Film: *Star Wars*.
1979	Shah of Iran deposed. Margaret Thatcher elected British Prime Minister. Soviet invasion of Afghanistan.	Kaye, *The Far Pavilions*. Film: *Apocalypse Now*.
1980	Ronald Reagan elected US President. Polish trade union Solidarity formed. Iran-Iraq war begins	Wolfe, *The Right Stuff*. Film: *Raging Bull*.

Further Reading

Tito has not been particularly well served by biographers. The most comprehensive English-language biography is Jasper Ridley's (1994), which is readable and full of diligently-researched detail. The inevitable shortcoming of this book is that the worst chapters of Yugoslavia's demise had yet to occur at the time of writing, so that Tito's life is not viewed in full perspective. This is likely to be remedied by a forthcoming biography by Ivo Banac, the eminent Croatian historian currently teaching at Harvard, which could well become the definitive work.

Earlier works are a mixed bag. *Tito Speaks* by Vladimir Dedijer (1953) is perhaps the best of Dedijer's authorised biographical works on Tito. Dedijer, a Serbian journalist, was a confidant of Tito, and at one stage served on the Central Committee, so his view is hardly a dissident one (although he and Tito did briefly argue over the Djilas affair in the 1950s). Nevertheless, the book is one of the few useful sources on Tito's youth, which is why it is quoted extensively in the earlier chapters of this book. Tito's extensive dictation to Dedijer is often inaccurate when checked against historical record, and in other places seeks to present his early life as a piece with his later life, a revolutionary journey. But viewed with a discriminating eye, it is an adsorbing and entertaining read.

During Tito's life left-wing admirers in the West produced hagiographic biographies, including Zilliacus (1952) and Auty (1972). These are of limited factual value, glossing over various atrocities and wives, but make amusing period pieces.

More out of comradeship and friendship than sycophancy, the

British soldier Fitzroy Maclean also gave Tito the benefit of the doubt in works such as *Eastern Approaches* (1950) and *Disputed Barricades* (1957). These books read like Boys' Own adventure stories – and it must be said that the reality of Tito's life did indeed have a romping, Boys' Own quality at times.

The novelist Evelyn Waugh also dealt with Tito during the war, but did not form the same favourable impression as Maclean. His diaries (1979) include scurrilous and very funny periods in Yugoslavia, which in places deal directly with Tito.

After Tito repudiated his lieutenant Milovan Djilas, the latter produced several works highly critical of Tito. These are interesting not least because of Djilas's close personal and political association with Tito until the mid-1950s, although of course Djilas's personal motivations need to be borne in mind. The most easily available is *Tito: The Story from Inside* (1981).

Although not strictly a biography, Nora Beloff's *Tito's Flawed Legacy* (1985) is a brilliant polemical analysis of post-Tito, pre-implosion Yugoslavia during the 1980s. Beloff's analysis is incisive, detailed and compelling. It is not kind to Tito, but is perhaps a necessary antidote to the much more numerous laudatory works. More recently Stevan K Pavlowitch produced the concise and closely argued *Tito: Yugoslavia's Great Dictator: A Reassesment* (1993) which again is not very favourable. This book, however, assumes considerable existing background knowledge of Yugoslav history.

In terms of the context of Tito's life, a number of rigorous but accessible books aimed at non-expert readers have been published in recent years. These include Misha Glenny's *The Balkans* (1999) which takes on the huge task of chronicling the entire region from 1878 to the mid-1990s. At the level of the republics and provinces of Yugoslavia, *The Serbs* (2000) by Tim Judah and Noel Malcolm's *Kosovo* (1999) and *Bosnia* (1994) are all excellent. The biography of an individual leader, Adam Lebor's *Milošević* (2002), provides an excellent narrative of the implosion of Yugoslavia after Tito.

Finaly, no one who is interested in Yugoslavia should miss *Black Lamb and Grey Falcon* (1941) by Rebecca West. This massive Yugoslav travelogue was written in the late 1930s, and is eccentric, brilliant and funny. West was a fervent admirer of the Serbs, and does not disguise this in the text. Tito makes only a fleeting appearance, when a Scottish manager at the Trebča a mine in Kosovo names him as a mysterious Comintern labour agitator. But for a background understanding of the charms, feuds and passions of Yugoslavia, there is no better choice.

Acknowledgements

Slobodan Marković, Peter Vančura, Adam Lebor, Elena Cutting and Benedict King helped enormously by reading drafts and making useful suggestions. Sašo Podobnik in Ljubljana and Aleks Brkić in Belgrade were ideal fixers and collaborators. Sources in the former Yugoslavia – some of whose names are in the text but are too many to list here – were generous with their time, hospitality and memories, Gregor Roy Chaudhury was equally generous and hospitable in providing a place to work. Everything would have been much more difficult without the kind co-operation of the Cental European University library in Budapest. My agent Chelsey Fox deserves thanks for her support and confidence in me, as does the publisher, Barbara Schwepcke. Of course any errors are my own.

Picture Sources

The author and publishers wish to express their thanks to the following sources of illustrative material and/or permission to reproduce it. They will make the proper acknowledgements in future editions in the event that any omissions have occurred.

Akg – Images, London: pp. iii, v, vi, 53, 64, 77; Neil Barnett: pp. 3, 17, 134; Croatian National Museum: pp. 71, 75; Getty Images: pp. 10, 37, 43, 47, 57, 60, 68, 85, 111, 114, 119, 139; Topham Picturepoint: pp. 23, 83, 89, 95, 98, 103, 105, 108, 142, 145, 149.

Index

LIFE & TIMES FROM HAUS

Alexander the Great
by Nigel Cawthorne
'moves through the career at a brisk,
dependable canter in his pocket
biography for Haus.'
BOYD TONKIN, The Independent
ISBN 1-904341-56-X (pb) £9.99

Armstrong
by David Bradbury
'it is a fine and well-researched
introduction'
GEORGE MELLY Daily Mail
ISBN 1-904341-46-2 (pb) £8.99

Bach
by Martin Geck
'The production values of the book
are exquisite.' Guardian
ISBN 1-904341-16-0 (pb) £8.99
ISBN 1-904341-35-7 (hb) £12.99

Beethoven
by Martin Geck
'...this little gem is a truly handy
reference.' Musical Opinion
ISBN 1-904341-00-4 (pb) £8.99
ISBN 1-904341-03-9 (hb) £12.99

Bette Davis
by Laura Moser
'The author compellingly unearths
the complex, self-destructive woman
that lay beneath the steely persona
of one of the best-loved actresses of
all time.'
ISBN 1-904341-48-9 (pb) £9.99

Bevan
by Clare Beckett
and Francis Beckett
"Haus, the enterprising new
imprint, adds another name to its
list of short biographies ... a timely
contribution.'
GREG NEALE, BBC History
ISBN 1-904341-63-2 (pb) £9.99

Brahms
by Hans A Neunzig
'These handy volumes fill a gap in
the market for readable,
comprehensive and attractively
priced biographies admirably.'
JULIAN HAYLOCK, Classic fm
ISBN 1-904341-17-9 (pb) £8.99

Caravaggio
by Patrick Hunt
'a first-class, succinct but comprehensive,
introduction to the artist'
BRIAN TOVEY The Art Newspaper
ISBN 1-904341-73-X (pb) £9.99
ISBN 1-904341-74-8 (hb) £12.99

Churchill
by Sebastian Haffner
'one of the most brilliant things of
any length written about Churchill'
TLS
ISBN 1-904341-07-1 (pb) £9.99
ISBN 1-904341-49-7 (CD) £12.95
ISBN 1-904341-43-8 (AC) £12.95

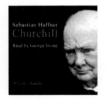

Curie
by Sarah Dry
'... this book could hardly be bettered'
New Scientist
selected as
Outstanding Academic Title by Choice
ISBN 1-904341-29-2 (pb) £8.99

Dali
by Linde Salber
'a fascinating view on this flamboyant
artist, the central and most excentric figure
in Surrealism, seen through the prism
of psychological analysis'
ISBN 1-904341-75-6 (pb) £9.99

De Gaulle
by Julian Jackson
'this concise and distinguished book'
Sunday Telegraph
ISBN 1-904341-44-6 (pb) £9.99

Dostoevsky
by Richard Freeborn
'wonderful ... a learned guide'
JOHN CAREY The Sunday Times
ISBN 1-904341-27-6 (pb) £8.99

Dvořák
by Kurt Honolka
'This book seems really excellent to me.'
SIR CHARLES MACKERRAS
ISBN 1-904341-52-7 (pb) £9.99

Einstein
by Peter D Smith
'Concise, complete, well-produced and
lively throughout, ... a bargain at the
price.' New Scientist
ISBN 1-904341-14-4 (hb) £12.99
ISBN 1-904341-15-2 (pb) £8.99

Gershwin
by Ruth Leon
'Musical theatre aficionados will relish
Ruth Leon's GERSHWIN, a succinct
but substantial account of the great composer's
life'
MICHAEL ARDITTI, The Independent
ISBN 1-904341-23-3 (pb) £9.99

Johnson
by Timothy Wilson Smith
'from a prize-winning author a biography
of the famous and perennially fascinating
figure, Samuel Johnson'
ISBN 1-904341-81-0 (pb) £9.99

Joyce
by Ian Pindar
'I enjoyed the book very much, and
much approve of this skilful kind of popularisation.
It reads wonderfully well.'
TERRY EAGLETON
ISBN 1-904341-58-6 (pb) £9.99

Kafka
by Klaus Wagenbach
'one of the most useful books on Kafka
ever published.' New Scientist
ISBN 1-904341-01-2 (hb) £12.99
ISBN 1-904341-02-0 (pb) £8.99

Moreschi, The Last Castrato
by Nicholas Clapton
'an immaculately produced and beautifully
illustrated short volume ... Clapton
is excellent on the physical and psychological
effects of castration as experienced
by Moreschi.'
ANDREW GREEN, Classical Music
ISBN 1-904341-77-2 (pb) £9.99

Mosley
by Nigel Jones
'an excellent brief life of Britain's 1930s
Fascist leader ... Jones does manage to get
a more accurate view of Mosley than some
previous, weightier books.'
FRANCIS BECKETT, Jewish Chronicle
ISBN 1-904341-09-8 (pb) £9.99

Nasser
by Anne Alexander
ISBN 1-904341-83-7 (pb) £9.99
Trotsky
by David Renton
ISBN 1-904341-62-4 (pb) £9.99

Trotsky
by David Renton
ISBN 1-904341-62-4 (pb) £9.99